Witnessing Like **PAUL**

XULON PRESS

Witnessing Like **PAUL**

JJ LUSK

Xulon Press
2301 Lucien Way #415
Maitland, FL 32751
407.339.4217
www.xulonpress.com

Unless otherwise indicated, Scripture quotations taken from the King James Version. Public domain.

Printed in the United States of America.

ISBN-13: 978-1-54566-934-1

Contents

—⟋⟍—

Acknowledgments

—ɱ—

First, I want to thank God for my amazing wife, Lindsay, without whom you wouldn't be reading any of this, as she was the first to encourage me to make this work and others available. Thank you dear. I can't imagine, nor would I be interested, in doing life without you.

I also owe a great debt to the people of Forest Hills, upon whom I "perfected" this series over the course of three years. Your patience and perseverance are truly inspiring.

Thanks also to the friends that either sat under my attempts to teach this series, taught it themselves, or merely read and commented on the manuscript. Your feedback has been invaluable.

Last but not least, I want to thank my wonderful graphic designer, Kristen King. You are truly an artisan at your craft! Without your work, people likely wouldn't give this book the time of day, but the cover is really cool!

Now, on to the introduction…

Introduction

Witnessing Like Paul was not written in a vacuum. It's not as though there aren't plenty of great works out there on the subject of witnessing, many of which are from far greater witnesses than I would ever claim to be. I am not that great.

The series was born purely out of my study of the apostle Paul. Our church has been going through the book of Acts for over four years. It has been the greatest and most personally beneficial study of my entire life, and in my opinion, has been the key to the health and the growth of our church. Throughout that series, I have become enamored with Paul and the way God used him to reach people and impact the world with the gospel.

Reading the account of his work in Acts and then comparing it to his letters to the churches he started fascinated me. Throughout that study, certain characteristics about Paul and his approach to reaching others began to stand out to me. Probably the most encouraging of which has been his humility regarding his humanity. Paul was just a man, and no one was more aware of that fact than he. Yet, God used him to altogether alter the very course of human history.

I have said to our church many times that the same God that worked through Paul to rock his generation with the gospel is the same God that is at work today. It is my opinion that if God did it then, He could do it again. If He did it through Paul, He could do it through you or me. Whether He does is up to Him, but He could, and that's how all of this began. If God is the same, was there something unique about Paul?

I started making notes as I continued to read through the book of Acts and Paul's letters. At some point, I decided to try to organize everything in such a way that I could begin to teach it to our church, and thus the *Witnessing Like Paul* series was born. That is, after all, what the entire series has stemmed from, simply watching Paul witness.

Though it is complete, it is by no means exhaustive. There is more that I may add at some point, but I feel it is sufficient as it is. It does the job, so to speak. It's a regular part of the spiritual diet of our church, and it's common for us to go through the series at least once a year.

You may notice the series is divided into sections rather than lessons. That's because each person is different. For me, trying to make it through a section in one teaching session was a joke. For others, it may be easy. I simply didn't want to set any unrealistic expectations at the outset. Take as much time as your folks need to grasp the content. That is, of course, the most important thing.

In line with this point, please understand this is not a book, but a study. Again, I put this together to teach, and so the format is such that it would lend itself to teaching. Because of that, I would highly recommend the student edition as well. I am convinced, and research supports, that retention is heightened when people write what they hear. Knowing there are blanks to fill in causes them to listen more intently for the word or phrase that fits. The student edition is a fill-in-the-blank resource to be used in conjunction with the teacher edition so that your audience better retains the content. This is the approach I have taken each time with our church, and it has worked well for us. Everywhere you see a word or phrase that is bold, italicized, and underlined, know that that phrase or word is a blank in the student edition that needs to be filled in.

My hope is that God would work through this series to develop within the hearts and minds of His people the same characteristics that I believe set Paul apart, that telling others about the wonderful love of God would become as natural to us as breathing, and that through it all, we would not only see fruit, but fruit that remains. Jesus is more than a fire escape. The focal point of the gospel is Him, not us. May He be lifted up that He might draw all men unto Himself!

WITNESSING LIKE PAUL – SECTION 1

Who Was the Apostle Paul?

—⚬⚬—

Section Aim

Section one is designed to help you become better acquainted with Paul, who he was, what God did in him, and what God did through him, so that you can see why such a study might be worth your time.

Who Was the Apostle Paul?

"But this one thing I do, forgetting those things which are behind, and reaching forth unto those things which are before, I press toward the mark for the prize of the high calling of God in Christ Jesus."
Paul the Apostle

"The Conversion of Saul of Tarsus, the leading persecutor of the Christians, was perhaps the greatest event in church history after the coming of the Spirit at Pentecost."[1]
Warren Wiersbe

Who Was the Apostle Paul?

First, just to be clear, we're talking about Paul the apostle. In my opinion, he is God's replacement for Judas Iscariot as one of the twelve, but that is a topic for another study perhaps. Paul is referred to as the apostle to the Gentiles. As you will see throughout this study, he had a heart for his people, the children of Israel and regularly took the gospel to them first anytime he reached a new city or town, but the spread of the gospel to the rest of the Gentile world is largely due to Paul's efforts. In his lifetime he took the gospel throughout Asia Minor into the regions of Syria and Cilicia, Cappadocia, Galatia, Pisidia, Asia, Mysia, and then on into Macedonia and Achaia, with ambitions of going into other areas such as Bithynia and Spain. A testament (no pun intended) to the impact Paul had on his world is the fact that much of the New Testament is comprised of letters written by him to groups of people that he reached in these areas during his missionary or evangelistic work. That includes the letters to the Galatians, the Ephesians, the Philippians, the Colossians, both letters to the Thessalonians, both letters to the Corinthians, and in my opinion, the letter to the Hebrews. He also wrote the letter to the Romans, a letter to Titus and to Philemon, and he wrote two letters to Timothy, but the first list is comprised of letters written by Paul to groups of people that he personally reached with the gospel. If you are a Gentile, (if you aren't Jewish, that's you) and you have heard the gospel, it isn't a stretch to say that you have Paul to thank.

So, with that in mind, who is Paul, and why will we be spending our time together in this study learning to witness like him?

- He was a Hebrew and a Roman citizen. –***Acts 22:24-28***

NOTE: Apparently, Claudius Lysias had obtained his Roman citizenship through bribery, but Paul was born a citizen of Rome. At some point, someone in Paul's family obtained citizenship, enabling Paul to be born free.

By the way, Claudius Lysias is a man first mentioned in Acts 21:31, and referred to merely as, "the chief captain of the band." We aren't given his name until Acts 23:26. He was a Roman commander of around 600-1,000 troops stationed near the temple in Jerusalem. He rescued Paul from a Jewish mob that apprehended him in the temple. The mob would have killed Paul had Claudius not stepped in. After trying to better understand what the uproar was about by allowing both Paul and his accusers to speak for themselves, he eventually sent Paul to Caesarea of Palestine to appear before Felix, the

Roman procurator or governor at that time. Claudius Lysias was not born a Roman citizen, but likely acquired his citizenship at a fee.[2,3]

    o Paul's Roman citizenship came in handy on at least a few different occasions.
- Acts 16:35-39
- Acts 22:24-30
- Acts 25:10-12

    o Of course, the fact that he was beaten repeatedly by many would seem to indicate that not everyone was impressed by it or cared (2 Corinthians 11:24-25).

- Paul was born in Tarsus, a city of Cilicia, around 4 AD. –Acts 21:39
- He was an ***educated*** man.

    o Paul could speak at least ***three*** languages: Hebrew, Aramaic, and Greek (his ability to get along well in Rome and his desire to go there, as well as Spain, would suggest that he could possibly speak Latin as well).[4]

    o He could read Greek and quoted Greek poets, philosophers, and writers.
- Aratus, Greek poet –Acts 17:28
- Menander, Greek comic poet and writer –***1 Corinthians 15:33***
- Epimenides, Greek Stoic Philosopher – Titus 1:12
- He reads the Greek inscription in Athens, "To The Unknown God" –Acts 17:23

- Paul was a **_tentmaker_** by trade (Acts 18:3), which basically meant he was a leather worker.
- He was, apparently, a bit of a sports fan, often using sports analogies in his writing.
  - o 2 Timothy 2:5
  - o 1 Corinthians 9:24–27 (each verse has its own athletic illustration).
  - o **_1 Timothy 4:8_**
  - o 2 Timothy 4:7
  - o Hebrews 12:1-2 (it is my opinion that Paul wrote Hebrews).

And as you will see. . .

- He was a passionate person.
  - o He wasn't the kind of guy that was half-hearted about anything he did.
  - o He was all in, no matter what.

- **_Judaism_** was his religion.
  - o As a Pharisee, he was trained at the feet of Gamaliel. –Acts 22:1-3

NOTE: Acts 5:34 helps us to see the great influence of Gamaliel. Gamaliel is considered, historically, as one of the greatest rabbinical scholars of all time.

  - o Paul lists his own credentials as a Jew in **_Philippians 3:4-6._**
    - ■ Circumcised the eighth day according to the law.
    - ■ Of the stock, or lineage, of Israel.

- Of the tribe of ***Benjamin***.
- A Hebrew of the Hebrews.
- A Pharisee.
- Zealous persecutor of churches and followers of Jesus.
- ***Blameless*** regarding the righteousness of the law.

NOTE: Wiersbe says of Paul's resume:

He was born into a pure Hebrew family and entered into a covenantal relationship when he was circumcised. He was not a proselyte, nor was he descended from Ishmael (Abraham's other son) or Esau (Isaac's other son) ... Benjamin and Joseph were Jacob's favorite sons. They were born to Rachel, Jacob's favorite wife. Israel's first king came from Benjamin, and this little tribe was faithful to David during the rebellion under Absalom. Paul's human heritage was something to be proud of![5]

   o As a devout Jew and Pharisee, Paul ***hated*** Jesus, His claims, and His followers, and zealously ***persecuted*** them more than any other Jew of his day.

      ■ ***Galatians 1:13-14***: "For ye have heard of my conversation in time past in the Jews' religion, how that beyond measure I persecuted the church of God, and wasted it: And profited in the Jews' religion above many my equals in mine own nation, being more exceedingly zealous of the traditions of my fathers."

      ■ 1 Timothy 1:13: "Who was before a blasphemer, and a persecutor, and injurious: but I obtained mercy, because I did [it] ignorantly in unbelief."

- Acts 8:3: "As for Saul, he made havock of the church, entering into every house, and haling men and women committed them to prison."

NOTE: A testament to the truth of Paul's statement in Galatians 1:14 regarding his zeal far exceeding that of his peers can be seen in Acts 8:3. Few would have persecuted *__women__* to the same extent as they would have persecuted *__men__*, but Paul did. When Luke says that Paul haled men and women, it means that he dragged them. He would go into their homes, grab them, and literally drag them out.

I have often wondered what it was like for Paul to go back to the Jerusalem church as a believer. I wonder if he battled guilt or felt shame. There were families that had been decimated due to his persecution. No doubt there were children in that church that had watched Paul arrest their parents. Now they see him come back as a believer, and even as a leader.

- Acts 22:4: "And I persecuted this way unto the death, binding and delivering into prisons both men and women."
- Acts 22:20: "And when the blood of thy martyr Stephen was shed, I also was standing by, and consenting unto his death, and kept the raiment of them that slew him."
- *__Acts 26:9-10__*:

I verily thought with myself, that I ought to do many things contrary to the name of Jesus of Nazareth. Which thing I also did in Jerusalem: and many of the saints did I shut up in prison, having received authority from the chief priests; and when they were put to death, I gave my voice against [them].

- ■ Acts 26:11: "And I punished them oft in every synagogue, and compelled [them] to blaspheme; and being exceedingly mad against them, I persecuted [them] even unto strange cities."

Eventually Paul became a follower of Jesus, and Jesus changed his life.

Understanding what we do about Saul of Tarsus, you can see how this is a big deal.

- • Consider again his own testimony of how he persecuted churches and those that followed this Jesus of Nazareth.

NOTE: It might be that the reason you aren't inclined to witness to those around you is because you are convinced they'll never humble their hearts and trust in Christ. If Paul's testimony teaches us anything, it's that you simply ***cannot*** write someone off regardless of how ***difficult*** they are or how ***opposed*** to the gospel they seem to be. After all, Paul persecuted Christians for around three years and maybe longer before he trusted Christ.

- • Luke records in Acts 2, what is possibly the point at which the Holy Spirit ***began convicting*** Saul (whether it was his first exposure to the message of the gospel, we don't know).
  - o He probably heard Peter preach on the day of Pentecost.

o He was a devout Jew and a Pharisee – Acts 2:5.

NOTE: It's interesting because, I now live in Rockville, Maryland. In my city there is quite a large Jewish population. I have several friends that are Jewish, and it is common for them to go back to Israel during the times of the feasts. They still do that even to this day.

o Even as a Christian Paul was eager to return to Jerusalem to keep the feasts – Acts 20:16.

o When you compare Peter's message in Acts 2 to Paul's message in Acts 13:17–41, you can see the similarities between the two, especially in regard to the prophecies of David.

o So, it's not a stretch to consider that Paul was likely there when Peter preached, in Acts 2, one of the most powerful gospel messages a Hebrew could have heard.

• In Acts 7, as he presides over the execution of **_Stephen_**, Saul was exposed to another powerful Gospel message by none other than Stephen himself.

o This time, not only was the gospel preached, but Jesus is presented as the 'Just One' of Israel (v.52).

o The term 'Just One' was synonymous with the 'Righteous Servant' mentioned throughout Old Testament prophecy regarding the Messiah – Isaiah 53:11; Jeremiah 23:5; 33:15

o Paul knew exactly what Stephen was saying.

o Stephen also charged the children of Israel, including the crowd standing before him, with constantly, throughout their entire history, resisting the Holy Ghost of God and persecuting and slaying His prophets who foretold of this Just One.

And then. . .

o He goes on to charge them of now betraying and murdering the ***Just One*** of which they prophesied!

o I think this message was particularly impactful for Paul because, though Paul was a man of action and a man of passion, he was also a man of reason as we see throughout his ministry in his writing and his preaching.

o This was a well-reasoned case that Stephen made.

o And then there is the testimony of Stephen that accompanied his message.

o Stephen accepted his fate with courage, grace, and mercy.

o No doubt Paul witnessed this sort of thing over and over as he persecuted Jesus' disciples.

NOTE: I think it's worth noting that both Peter and Stephen presented arguments for Jesus that were solid and substantive. These weren't merely emotional pleas, nor were they efforts to play on fear. They reasoned with Paul, a man of reason, and he was convicted ...

• Acts 9 is the record of Saul's ***conversion*** where Jesus indicates that Saul was already battling conviction within.

- o The "pricks" like an ox goad were stabbing at his heart. –Acts 9:5
- o Basically, this encounter served to confirm the suspicions already present in Saul's heart – that Jesus is the Messiah after all.
- o So, he humbles his heart and puts his trust in Jesus as the ***Christ***!

NOTE: An interesting thought here is in the way Paul uses the word, 'Lord' in his exchange with Jesus. In Acts 9:5, when Paul uses the title, it is simply a matter of what you might call cautious respect. He doesn't know who he is talking to. He doesn't know what is going on. He doesn't know if this is some elaborate trick, or if he is dealing with some truly imposing individual. All he knows is that whoever it is, they know him. So, he plays it safe.

The second time he uses the title, in v.6, he knows exactly who he is talking to. Saul, the man of whom Luke says threatenings and slaughter toward Christians was his very life's breath (Acts 9:1), would have never referred to Jesus as Lord...

Something had changed.

- • According to Luke's account and Paul's personal testimony, things were not the same; he was not the same!
  - o Acts 9:17–20: the next thing we read about Saul is that he is in the synagogue preaching, trying to help other Jews understand who Jesus is.
    - ▪ Before he trusted Christ, he "thought ... that [he] ought to do many things ***contrary*** to the name of Jesus of Nazareth." –Acts 26:9

11

- After he trusted Christ, his perspective changed: "*__Christ__* Jesus came into the world to save sinners; of whom I am chief." –1 Timothy 1:15

After Paul began to follow Jesus, he gave his life to the effort of telling others about Him.

- Romans 15:20–21: "Yea, so have I *__strived__* to preach the gospel, not where Christ was named, lest I should build upon another man's foundation: But as it is written, to whom he was not spoken of, they shall see: and they that have not heard shall understand."
  - o Paul wrote the letter to the Romans during his third missionary journey.
  - o By this point he was likely already in his *__fifties__* and apparently had no plans of slowing down.
  - o Dave Hardy, a Christian man whom I admire greatly, once said (explaining why he continues to still go to the reunions for the submarine he served on in the Navy), "There is still a harvest field for me there."
  - o I imagine if someone asked Paul as he got older, "Why don't you give it a rest and let someone else take over now?", that he would say something similar: *__"There is still a harvest for me__.*"

- Paul would write in *__1 Corinthians 9:16__*, "For though I preach the gospel, I have nothing to glory of: for necessity is laid upon me; yea, woe is unto me, if I preach not the gospel!"

o   It's like Paul is saying, *Yes. I do actually preach the gospel, but I can't brag about that. I simply can't help it.*

o   Necessity means "constraint", and woe means "grief".

*So, that's who Paul was—a **normal**, and perhaps in some ways exceptional, **person** who became a follower of Jesus and gave his life to the effort of telling others about Him.*

Now, why are we going to spend the next few weeks trying to learn how to witness like him?

Because…

The impact God had on this world through him can hardly be measured.

David Thomas said the conversion of the apostle Paul was one of the:

> Greatest facts that has ever occurred in the history of God's redemptive providence. The thirty years of his ministry … threw the ideas of Jesus with a force into the heart of the world, that shattered old systems, and established everywhere those organizations called "churches" which have been multiplying ever since, and which are destined to work a moral revolution in the world. It has been said, obliterate from the world the influence of this man's thirty years' ministry, and you sweep away all churches from the face of the earth, you quench the moral lights of the age, you give back Ephesus to Diana, Athens to Minerva, Paphos to Venus, Rome to all the

gods of her pantheon, and plunge the whole world once more into pagan darkness and heathen dissoluteness.[6]

With that in mind, I think it's easy to see that we can perhaps learn a thing or two.

Different characteristics of the apostle Paul that we are going to be taking a closer look at include:

- Paul's heart for the ***lost***.
- Paul's tremendous ***faith*** in ***God*** and the gospel and his healthy perspective regarding the latter (he was a debtor).
- Paul's ***contextually sensitive*** and flexible approach; in other words, he knew the people he preached to as well as he knew the gospel he preached and presented it in a way that it spoke to their particular context.
- Paul's method for presenting the gospel: Paul didn't just declare (though he did indeed declare with confidence, which is also important), he also patiently ***reasoned***, disputed, ***persuaded***, and testified.

And finally. . .

- Paul's knowledge of the God of creation, the gospel of that God, and the Jesus of that Gospel—he ***mastered*** this subject matter; he knew his business.

Conclusion:

Our world today has more people in it than it has ever had before. It would seem logical then, especially in light of the diminished influence of biblical Christianity, that there are more lost people in it than there have ever been before. Now, more than ever, we need men and women to witness.

- We need people who have become followers of Jesus to give themselves to the effort of telling others about Him and sharing the gospel with everyone, everywhere.
- We need people who will have a heart for the lost, a tremendous faith in God and the gospel, a right perspective regarding the gospel, and a contextually sensitive and flexible approach to presenting the gospel.
- We need men and women who will declare, and who will reason, and who will dispute, and who will persuade, and who will testify, and who will do so patiently and with love!
- We need men and women who will know God, the gospel, and Jesus both practically and academically — people who will master that subject matter.

We need people who will *Witness . . . Like Paul . . .*

WITNESSING LIKE PAUL – SECTION 2

Paul Had a Heart for the Lost!

—∽—

Section Aim

The purpose of section two is introspection. When considering Paul's heart for lost people, how do we look in comparison?

Paul Had a Heart for the Lost!

*If sinners will be damned, at least let them leap to hell over
our bodies. And if they will perish, let them perish with our
arms about their knees, imploring them to stay. If hell must
be filled, at least let it be filled in the teeth of our exertions,
and let not one go there unwarned and unprayed for.[7]*
Charles Haddon Spurgeon

*"What a man this Paul was! He was willing to stay out of
Heaven for the saved (Phil. 1:22–24), and willing to go to
Hell for the sake of the lost (Rom. 9:1–3)."[8]*
Warren Wiersbe

Consider the strength of Paul's words in the book of Romans.

- Romans 9:1–4a: *"I say the truth in Christ, I lie not, my
  conscience also bearing me witness in the Holy Ghost,
  That I have **great heaviness** and **continual sorrow in
  my heart**. For I could wish that myself were **accursed
  from Christ** for my brethren, my kinsmen according to
  the flesh: Who are Israelites. . ."*
  - o Paul had great heaviness and sorrow continually in
    his heart for the lost.
    - Great heaviness: sorrow, pain, grief; it has to
      do with a person who is **mourning** in the same
      manner as one would for a loved one who
      passed away.
    - Continual sorrow: carries the same idea as
      "great heaviness", but **without ceasing**; contin-
      ually, unceasingly.

NOTE: Paul's sorrow for the lost wasn't something that came and went. It was something that weighed heavy upon his heart and mind ***always***.

- o His burden for the lost was so great that, if it were possible, he would give up his own salvation and spend the rest of eternity separated from Christ in hell, if it meant the salvation of others.
- o Accursed from Christ: separated from Christ; the Greek word is ***anathema*** and has the idea of being "doomed to destruction."[9]

- • Rom. 10:1: "Brethren, my heart's ***desire*** and ***prayer*** to God for Israel is, that they might be ***saved***."
  - o Paul's clear about the one thing that would bring him satisfaction: the salvation of the lost, and in particular, Israel.
    - ▪ Heart, *kardia*, literally the muscle that pumps blood through the body; figuratively, the center of one's being.
    - ▪ Desire: delight, pleasure, satisfaction.
  - o As Paul's desire is from the heart, so is his ***prayer***; he prays ***earnestly***, ***fervently*** for this one thing, "that they might be saved."

NOTE: It is like Paul is saying, "*I desire and pray with all that I am.*"

Paul's concern for lost souls knew no bounds.

The passages referenced above reveal that Paul's heart for the lost extended even to those who wished him **_harm_**.

* It was primarily the Jews that sought to harm Paul and interfere with the work he was doing even on their behalf.
    o **_Acts 9:23–24_**: Just after Paul's conversion, he began preaching, and the first place he went was the synagogue. Shortly thereafter, the Jews turned on him.
    o Again, we see the **_Jews_** in action against Paul in Acts 13:45, 50.
    o Over and again, the Jews cause **_trouble_** for Paul.
        ■ Acts 14:2–5: "But the unbelieving Jews stirred up the Gentiles, and made their minds evil affected against the brethren. ... And when there was an assault made both of the Gentiles, and also of the Jews with their rulers, to use them despitefully, and to stone them. . ."
        ■ Acts 14:19: "And there came thither certain Jews from Antioch and Iconium, who persuaded the people, and, having stoned Paul, drew him out of the city, supposing he had been dead."
        ■ Acts 17:5: "But the Jews which believed not, moved with envy, took unto them certain lewd fellows of the baser sort, and gathered a company, and set all the city on an uproar, and assaulted the house of Jason, and sought to bring them out to the people."
        ■ Acts 17:13: "But when the Jews of Thessalonica had knowledge that the word of God was

preached of Paul at Berea, they came thither also, and stirred up the people."

*This is the case throughout the book of **Acts**.*

- Yet, time and again Paul went to the **_Jew_** first; each time he went to a new city, the synagogue was the first place he would head.
  - o Just after being sent out of the church in Antioch to do the work God had for him. –Acts 13:5
  - o In verse 14 of the same chapter, we find them in another city and the first place they go is the **_synagogue_**.
  - o This pattern is seen throughout Paul's **_ministry_**.
    - ■ Acts 14:1: "And it came to pass in Iconium, that they went both together into the synagogue of the Jews, and so spake. . ."
    - ■ Acts 17:1–2: "Now when they had passed through Amphipolis and Apollonia, they came to Thessalonica, where was a synagogue of the Jews: And Paul, as his manner was, went in unto them, and three sabbath days reasoned with them out of the scriptures. . ."
    - ■ Acts 17:10: "And the brethren immediately sent away Paul and Silas by night unto Berea: who coming thither went into the synagogue of the Jews."
    - ■ Acts 17:16–17: "Now while Paul waited for them at Athens, his spirit was stirred in him, when he saw the city wholly given to idolatry.

> Therefore disputed he in the synagogue with the Jews. . ."

- Acts 18:4: "And he reasoned in the synagogue every sabbath, and persuaded the Jews and the Greeks."

*The list could go on. No matter how much they rejected the Lord and Paul, Paul **consistently went to the Jews** in an effort to reason with them from the Scriptures regarding Jesus of Nazareth.*

- They **plotted** against him, lied about him, caused others to hate him, beat him, had him arrested on more than one occasion, and tried on more than one occasion to **murder** him.
- These are the people that Paul said he would give up his **salvation** for if he could. By the way, when he wrote that in Romans, it was toward the end of his third and final missionary journey, and before they succeeded in having him arrested the final time, which would lead to his execution by Rome. So, most of what they would do, they had already done, and yet he still was willing to give up heaven if it meant they would trust in Jesus as the Christ.

Paul's heart for the lost truly knew **no bounds**.

Paul's heart for the lost is further demonstrated in his efforts to reach them.

- He completely gave his **life** to this effort.[10]

o   Paul traveled to and preached in at least *fifty-five* cities, and probably many more.

o   He went on at least three missionary journeys and one final journey to Rome. –Acts 13, 15:40, 18:23, chapters 27-28.

o   Many believe he did more work after his first Roman imprisonment between 63 and 65AD.

o   He traveled by foot, ship, and various other means at least *10,282* miles which took at least *281* days throughout the course of his *ten to eleven* years' worth of missionary journeys alone.

o   His total ministry spanned some thirty years.

o   Those travels cost him roughly *1,731* denarii, which in our currency would equate to about $*346,200.00* (much of which probably came from his own pocket).

o   While he was writing to the Romans from Corinth toward the end of his third missionary journey, Paul made it clear that he had no intentions of slowing down (Romans 15:15–24).

o   In fact, Rome, in Paul's mind, wasn't even his final destination.

o   It was just a stop on his way to Spain!

NOTE: Remember what we said before. By the time he wrote his letter to the Romans, he was already in his fifties.

He completely gave his *body* and well-being to this effort.

o   In Acts 14:19–20 (v.21: they returned to Lystra where Paul was just stoned), Paul is stoned, seemingly to death at Lystra.

o In Acts 16:23–24, Paul and Silas were whipped and thrown in prison.

o In Acts 21:13, Paul makes it clear that he is ready to be bound and, if necessary, die for Christ's sake.

o In 2 Corinthians 11:23-25, Paul lists some of the times he suffered in his effort to preach the gospel.

   ■ On at least five different occasions he received 39 lashes by the Jews.

   ■ On at least three different occasions he was beaten with rods.

   ■ Once he was stoned, which we read about above.

   ■ Three different times he was shipwrecked (not counting the time he was shipwrecked in Malta in Acts 27, because that hadn't happened yet).

   ■ During one of those shipwrecks, he spent at least one 24 hour period floating around in the sea.

   ■ Also, after writing this, he was beaten in Jerusalem by the Jews so badly he couldn't walk by himself (Acts 21:35).

o As if the specifics of 2 Corinthians 11:23-25 weren't enough, he then continues with a more general list of sufferings in vv.26-27:

In journeyings often, in perils of waters, in perils of robbers, in perils by mine own countrymen, in perils by the heathen, in perils in the city, in perils in the wilderness, in perils in the sea, in perils among false brethren; In weariness and painfulness, in watchings often, in hunger and thirst, in fastings often, in cold and nakedness. Beside those things that are without, that which cometh upon me daily, the **_care_** of all the **_churches_**.

Certainly, these lists of the ways in which Paul sacrificed himself physically for the sake of the gospel aren't exhaustive...

- He completely sacrificed his **reputation** to this effort.
  - o He was a **Jew**.
  - o He was a Pharisee of the Pharisees.
  - o He was feared.
  - o He was respected (Galatians 1:14).
  - o Yet, because of his work to spread the gospel of Jesus, he was **mocked**, falsely accused, imprisoned, **slandered**, misrepresented, and more.
  - o No longer would he be respected among the Jewish elite.
    - Acts 9:20–21: "But all that heard him were amazed, and said; **Is not this he** that destroyed them which called on this name in Jerusalem, and came hither for that intent, that he might bring them bound unto the chief priests?"
    - Acts 14:19: "And there came thither certain Jews from Antioch and Iconium, who **persuaded the people**, and, having stoned Paul. . ."
    - **Acts 17:4–6**:

But the Jews which believed not, moved with envy, took unto them certain lewd fellows of the baser sort, and gathered a company, and set all the city on an uproar. … they drew Jason and certain brethren unto the rulers of the city, crying, "These that have turned the world upside down are come hither also."

NOTE: According to the Jews, Paul had earned the reputation of being a ***troublemaker***. This was, apparently, how he was known among his countrymen. That is the idea behind the phrase, "turned the world upside down."

- Acts 17:32: "And when they heard of the resurrection of the dead, some ***mocked*. . ."
- Acts 21:27–31: Apprehended in Jerusalem.
- Acts 24:1–9: On trial.

NOTE: It's important to consider, regarding the many times he was arrested, the image that gives a person in the eyes of the general public. His reputation was potentially tarnished before he ever got a chance with some people.

- Acts 26:24: "And as he thus spake for himself, Festus said with a loud voice, 'Paul, thou art beside thyself; much learning doth make thee ***mad***.'"

Paul gave everything to the effort of telling people how much God loved them and inviting them to put their faith and trust in Him through Christ. He did so, not just out of duty or obligation, but because he genuinely cared for the lost.

Conclusion:

Spurgeon once said:

Every true Christian should be exceedingly earnest in prayer concerning the souls of the ungodly, and when they are so, how abundantly God blesses them, and how much the church prospers. But beloved, souls may be damned, yet how few of you care about them! Sinners may sink into perdition, yet how few tears are shed over them! The whole world may be swept away by a torrent down the precipice of woe, yet how few really cry to God on its behalf. How few men say, "Oh that my head were waters and mine eyes a fountain of tears, that I may weep day and night for the slain of the daughter of my people!" (Jer. 9:1). We do not lament before God the loss of men's souls, as it well becomes Christians to do.[11]

I think briefly two ways to strengthen one's burden for the lost is to first ***pray*** for that burden and for the lost. Pray for both regularly. The second is to begin ***sharing*** the gospel. It is amazing how quickly rejection makes one aware of the genuine need that is out there.

Paul **utterly** spent himself in pursuit of lost souls. He had a heart for the lost.

With Paul's example in mind, consider that studies show "***eighty-two percent*** of the unchurched are at least 'somewhat likely' to attend church if they are invited."[12]

Thom Rainer makes a big deal of this finding. "Perhaps we need to pause on this response. Perhaps we need to restate it: *More than eight out of ten of the unchurched said they would come to church if they were invited.*"[13]

He then asks:

What constitutes an invitation? For many of the unchurched, it was a simple statement of invitation to come to one's church. For others, it was an invitation that included the offer to meet someone at church to show them around. In either case, the process was pretty basic. If we invite them, they will come.[14]

"The next obvious question is," he says, "Are Christians inviting non-Christians to church? The heartbreaking answer is no. Only ___two percent___ of active church goers invite *anyone* to church in the course of a year. But only ___two percent___ of church members invite an unchurched person to church."[15]

If that statistic holds true, just think of how much more dismal the number of believers out there talking to the unchurched specifically about Jesus must be...

Paul gave all that he was in his effort to get people to Jesus, and the average Christian isn't even willing to invite someone to church. I think we can learn something from Paul.

People said of John Wesley, that he was out of breath in pursuit of souls. This should be the defining statement of every believer, but it will not be so unless we develop a heart that is truly broken for the lost.

Paul: A Man of Proper Perspective and Great Faith!

—ɱ—

Section Aim

The purpose of section three is to give a sense of Paul's very healthy perspective regarding the gospel, as well as his faith in the gospel, so that we can possibly begin to develop that same **_boldness_** to preach with confidence to **_anyone_**, **_anywhere_**.

Paul: A Man of Proper Perspective and Great Faith!

"It made little difference to Paul whether a man was cultured or crude, an intellectual or an ignoramus. He would proclaim Christ with equal passion to a runaway slave like Onesimus or to a proud monarch like King Agrippa."[16]
John Phillips

"I am ready to preach the gospel to you that are at Rome also. For I am not ashamed of the gospel of Christ: for it is the power of God unto salvation to everyone that believeth; to the Jew first, and also to the Greek."[17]
The Apostle Paul

Paul was _bold_.

Key Text: **_Romans 1:14–16_**

- According to Google, the source of all knowledge in the millennial universe, the definition of the word "bold" is: "(of a person, action, or idea) showing an ability to take risks; confident and courageous."[18]
- Paul was bold.
- His boldness can be seen in our text in his use of the phrase, "**_I am ready_**. . ." in Romans 1:15.
  - o The phrase comes from a Greek word that is used only three times in the New Testament.
  - o It has the idea of being willing or predisposed, and really, predisposed is the more complete idea, meaning to arrange things beforehand.

- o The idea is that his mind was already made up; he was ready.
- o Regarding Paul's use of this phrase, John Phillips wrote:

Here was Paul's boldness… Paul was ready to preach the gospel at Rome. When he preached it at Jerusalem, the religious center of the world, he was mobbed. When he preached it at Athens, the intellectual center of the world, he was mocked. When he preached it at Rome, the legislative center of the world, he was martyred. ***He was ready for that****. He was ready to preach the gospel …*[19]

NOTE: It's like if you were to ask him, "What about (whatever)? What if you get arrested? What if they don't like what you have to say? What if they are not religious? What if they have a different religion? What about opposition?" He would say, "I am ready." He then would act in accordance with his inclination, his aptitude (his tendency). ***That is boldness****.*

- • Consider Paul's boldness communicated in other passages.
    - o Acts 20:22–24 and 21:11–13: after being warned repeatedly of what awaited him in Jerusalem, he went anyway ready for either bondage or death.
    - o It was Paul's hope and desire that Christ would be magnified in him even if it meant death (***Phil. 1:20***).

- No matter what he might encounter, Paul had determined already to move forward with the gospel anyway; that is boldness.
- It doesn't mean he wasn't afraid; it meant fear wasn't going to **_control_** or **_stop_** him.

NOTE: Boldness and arrogance are not synonymous. History is full of Christians that were both bold and humble. Paul is an example of this. The same man that said, "I am ready" is the same one that claimed to be chiefest of sinners.

So, Paul says, "I am ready." He had great boldness, but what was he ready to do?

Paul was ready to preach the gospel to anyone and everyone, anywhere and everywhere!

- The phrase "to preach the gospel" comes from one Greek word, *euaggelizo*: to **_bring_** good news; to **_announce_** good tidings.
- How do we know Paul was ready to preach the gospel to everyone, everywhere when, in verse 15, Paul mentions only **_Rome_**?
  - o Well, for starters, he says plainly in Romans 15:20-21, that his desire was to preach Christ where Christ had not been named.
  - o Secondly, we have record of him literally travelling all around the Mediterranean preaching the gospel everywhere he went.

but beyond that...

- o In the text, he doesn't say that he is ready to preach the gospel in Rome.
- o He says he is ready to preach in, "Rome **_also_**".
- o Paul is saying he is ready to preach the gospel in Rome as well.
- o He is ready to preach the gospel, period, and that includes in Rome.
- To get an accurate picture of who Paul was "ready" to reach with the gospel, we have to look at all three verses:
  - o The Jews: v.16
  - o The Greeks: v.14, 16
  - o **_The Barbarians_**: v.14

NOTE: Consider Vine's note regarding the word "Barbarian". He said it:

Properly meant "one whose speech is rude, or harsh;" the word is onomatopoeic, indicating in the sound the uncouth character represented by the repeated syllable "bar-bar." Hence it signified one who speaks a strange or foreign language. See 1 Corinthians 14:11. It then came to denote any foreigner ignorant of the Greek language and culture.

In addition to the Jews, the Greeks, and the Barbarians, Paul was ready to preach to:
- o The wise: v.14
- o The unwise: v.14
- o And those that were at Rome **_also_**.

33

- So, Paul was "ready" to preach, not just to the Jew or to the Greek, but to everyone, everywhere — even to those in Rome also!
  - o That is just six people groups, right?

How does that count as everyone?

  - o In the Jewish mind, if you weren't a Jew, you were Greek or a Gentile.
  - o Paul gets even more thorough and adds a few extra categories to make sure all the bases are covered:
    - ▪ Barbarians
    - ▪ Wise and unwise
    - ▪ Those at Rome.
  - o In the thinking of Paul's day, he covered ***all of mankind***.
    - ▪ He wasn't concerned with race at all!
    - ▪ Nor was he concerned with one's station in life.
    - ▪ None of that mattered to him!
  - o He was concerned about ***one*** thing only and that was ***preaching the gospel*** where it had not been preached and to those who had not heard it (Romans 15).
  - o He was "ready" no matter what or who stood before him!
- The boldness of Paul can be seen throughout the pages of the ***book of Acts***!
  - o Acts 9:20: Paul had not been saved long, and he heads into the ***synagogue*** to preach.

- ■ In fact, Luke describes this as Paul's manner: preaching to the Jews in the synagogues in each town that he visited.
- ■ Paul would even preach to the **_Sanhedrin_** while he stood on trial.
- o Acts 17:18–31: He preached to the thinkers and **_philosophers_** of his day, some of which mocked him.
- o **_Acts 20:21_**: Jews and Greeks (everyone—even Barbarians [Romans 1])
- o Acts 24:24–25: He preached to Felix; a crooked politician.
- o Acts 26:1–29: He preached to Festus and Agrippa; a governor and a king.
- o Acts 28:17–24: He preached to the chief Jews of Rome.
- o Acts 28:31: I think the last verse of the book of Acts stands as a representation of the apostle Paul's preaching as a whole: "with all **_confidence_**".

Now, before moving on, I want to explain, briefly, who Felix, Festus, and Agrippa are. I mentioned them in the outline above but feel it best to give some context so that you can appreciate their part in all of this. They are major players in the account.

Antonius Felix was a Roman procurator or governor of Judaea and Samaria. Claudius Lysias sent Paul to Felix so that perhaps Felix could figure out what to do with him. Felix has a "rags to riches" kind of a tale. He was at one time a slave who Claudius Caesar promoted to the office of governor. Virtually every historian I have read makes it clear that Felix was a vile man and a crooked politician. We are even told by Luke in Acts

24:26 that he was hoping that Paul would offer him a bribe for his release. He is first mentioned in Acts 23:24. He is replaced by Festus in Acts 25:14.[20]

Porcius Festus was the replacement to Antonius Felix as the governor of Judaea. He is the antithesis to Antonius. Felix was a corrupt politician. Festus was regarded as a wise and just official. Paul had been in prison under Felix for two years by the time Festus stepped into the picture. Festus basically inherited the situation with Paul, and the fact that he was a Roman meant that he had little understanding of what was taking place or even how to deal with it. That is made clear throughout the sections of Acts that include him. This is most evident in his desire to have King Agrippa hear Paul's case for the sake of helping Festus gain some perspective. It was before Festus that Paul made his appeal to Caesar that led to his first visit to Rome. Festus, though he didn't understand Paul or Paul's situation, was convinced that there was nothing laid to Paul's charge that was worthy of bonds or death. Nevertheless, he was bound to honor Paul's request to appeal to Caesar. Festus is first mentioned in Acts 24:27 and continues in the account until Acts 26:32.[21]

Last, but certainly not least, there is King Agrippa. He and Festus will both come up in this study again, and so it's good that you know who they are. King Herod Agrippa II is the great-grandson of Herod the Great, "the Jewish-Idumean leader who became a major client-king for the Romans" and ruled during Jesus birth.[22] Agrippa, as he is referred to in Acts 25-26, was the last of the Herodian dynasty and was also a client-king for the Romans. Because of Festus' ignorance in matters of Jewish tradition, when King Agrippa visited Caesarea, Festus sought his help in Paul's case. Agrippa was very familiar with and even identified with Jewish tradition as a Jewish king. Agrippa's kingdom basically consisted of several areas surrounding the Roman procuratorial ruled regions of Judaea and Samaria.[23,24,25]

This certainly helps you see the boldness of Paul. These men were some of the most powerful of their day in the regions over which they ruled, yet Paul bravely reached out to all with the gospel.

Read the book of Acts and watch as Paul, when he had a crowd in front of him, would "beckon with the hand" and begin to try to take advantage of the opportunity to help them understand _**who Jesus is**_ and His significance to them.

Just as John Phillips brilliantly points out in the aforementioned quote, Paul preached in Jerusalem, the _**religious**_ center of the world. He preached in Athens, the intellectual center of the world; and He preached in Rome, the _**legislative**_ center of the world. He would go anywhere and preach boldly to anyone.

So, I think it is evident that he was indeed ready. Paul had great boldness and would preach the gospel anywhere and to anyone!

"I am ready. . ."

So, where did Paul's boldness come from (other than the Spirit of God)?

Paul's boldness came from his perspective regarding the gospel and his faith in the gospel!

Which is something I am sure the Spirit of God helped him with.

We get this from our text in Romans 1:14-16.

- The wording of these three verses from our text shows a progression in thought where Paul's readiness is stated in between the two causes for it.
  o Paul says in v.14, "I am ___debtor___".
  o In v.15 he says, "<u>So</u>...I am ___ready___".
  o And in v.16, he says, "<u>For</u> I am not ___ashamed___".
  o The word "so" in v.15 has the idea of "because of" or "therefore", and the word "for" in v.16, has the idea of "because".
  o So, it's like Paul says, *I am debtor, therefore I am ready, because I am not ashamed.*
  o He was ready because, regarding the gospel, he understood himself to be a debtor, and, regarding the gospel, he was not ashamed.

*So, there were **two** reasons for Paul's boldness.*

- He saw himself as a debtor.
  o A debtor is one who is under an obligation or owes something to another.[26]
    ▪ There is no doubt in my mind that one element of his sense of indebtedness resulted from a sense of unworthiness on Paul's part.
    ▪ He knew who he was, meaning, in his mind, he was nothing special (something I love most about Paul; 1 Tim. 1:12–15).

Second Kings 7:3-9 illustrates this thinking: the idea of not hoarding good fortune, especially when received unworthily.

- However, the main purpose of Paul's use of the term "debtor" here has to do with the idea that he received the gospel for the purpose of giving it to others.
- He recognized that it was something that he had been entrusted with for the express purpose of delivering it to others and until those it was intended for received it, he was in ***their*** debt, he owed them (Acts 9:15).

NOTE: By the way, if you are wondering who it was intended for, consider our main text for this section. In Paul's mind, he was a debtor to everyone: the wise, the unwise, the Jew, the Greek, the Barbarian . . . everyone.

So, as much as in him was, he was ready—bold—because he was a debtor.

- He was also ready—bold—because he was not ***ashamed***.
  - o Ashamed: "reluctant or unwilling to do something because of shame or embarrassment."[27]

NOTE: That being said, I don't think it's the gospel that we tend to be ashamed of. I think it is mostly the image of Christianity within our culture. We know that some of it is unwarranted, but we also know that some of it is due to the way Jesus has been represented by people who claim to follow Him. Either way, we can't let that deter us.

I would imagine that it was the same in Paul's day as it is in ours. There were likely people that claimed to be Jesus' disciples that seemed to do their best to make following Jesus look as weird or absurd as possible. We may not want to be associated with that crowd of people, but Jesus is awesome! There is no one more loving. There is no one more kind. There is no one more gracious and patient. The Gospel is the story of God's perfect and just judgment being satisfied by His own immeasurable love. What is there to be ashamed of? We have to get over our concern with what people may think of us and take the gospel to them and look for opportunities to introduce them to Jesus.

By the way, if you think that the Jesus movement in Paul's day was looked at with any less disdain than in ours, just consider a few passages. First, take a look at Paul's time in Thessalonica. When they couldn't find Paul, they apprehended Jason and brought him before the magistrates. Now, pay attention to how they describe Christians: "these that have turned the world upside down... (Acts 17:6)." The phrase, "that have turned... upside down," comes from one Greek word that is translated in Galatians 5:12 as "trouble". The verse says, "I would they were even cut off which trouble you." The word on the street in Thessalonica regarding this sect was that they were troublemakers. That's what they had heard anyway. These people that have caused trouble in other places are here now. That's what they were saying. That was the reputation, regardless of whether it was just or not, of this movement back then.

Consider also Acts 28:17-22. Paul had made it to Rome. In Paul fashion, though his circumstances were perhaps different than he imagined they'd be, he began working on getting the gospel to people and trying to help them understand who Jesus is. God had made a way for him to do the work that he was passionate about in that Paul is granted a lot of liberty as a Roman prisoner. So, as his manner was, he begins with the

Jews. However, Paul has a few concerns. He is concerned about how they will view the fact that he is in prison. He is also concerned about what they may have heard about him. So, he has a group of Jewish leaders over to his home where he begins to explain his situation so that he can determine if there are going to be any obstacles to the gospel that he is going to need to overcome first. By the way, the work of repairing the image of Christianity in the eyes of the world is often a necessary first step that is overlooked by believers. Take it or leave it. Anyway, after he is done, he finds out that his fears regarding himself in this situation are unfounded. Consider, though, what the Jews say regarding the sect they know he is associated with. "But we desire to hear of thee what thou thinkest: for as concerning this sect, we know that every where it is spoken against (Acts 28:22)." Now, the cool thing is that they were curious to know more instead of being turned off by the reputation, but the reputation is clear. Christians were spoken against everywhere. So, you see? Paul refused to be deterred by the opinions of society regarding those following Jesus. We shouldn't let the opinions of society stop us either. Let's be ready to own our mistakes when necessary, but we can't be silent. The cost is too high.

- It may not be shame that is keeping you from trying to speak to others about the Lord.
- However, it may be, and you know if it is.
- Ask the Lord to help you with that.
o Paul was not ashamed of the gospel of Christ because it was the power of God unto salvation!
  - The Gospel represented God's power to save!
  - It was effective.

- The word for power is *dunamis* and it has to do with **_ability_**; like dynamite, it's powerful!
- It *is* able to deliver and save!
- It **_alone_** is able to deliver and save; one simply needs to hear and trust.

But . . .

- Not only is it able to deliver and save, it is able to convince.
- Paul was personally aware of this.
- Remember that when Jesus confronted him on the road to Damascus, he was already under conviction.

Paul knew firsthand what the gospel was capable of, and what **_God could do through the gospel_** *(1 Tim. 1:15). How could he be ashamed?*

So, Paul was ready to preach the gospel anywhere and everywhere, to anyone and everyone. He was bold. He was bold because of his perspective regarding the gospel and because of his faith in the gospel. That begs one question, and I believe it is a question modern day Christianity desperately needs to consider and answer, and that is . . .

What is the Gospel?

The reason I believe this section is so necessary is because the modern-day gospel seems very different from the one preached throughout the New Testament. We've taken something that is supposed to be all about God and Jesus, and we've made it all about us and heaven. "If you were to die today, are you sure you'd go to heaven? If you could know for sure that you were going to heaven, wouldn't you want to? Who wants to go to hell? Right? You don't have to go to hell. You can go to heaven." We wonder why people don't stick around after praying "the prayer." Perhaps it's because we've reinforced their thinking that life really is all about them. Even what we are calling the gospel centers on their preference of heaven over hell.

The gospel of the New Testament is very different. It doesn't center on man. It very much has God and Jesus as its focal point. In fact, the gospel itself is all about the love of God manifest through the incarnation, life, and death of His Son, Jesus, on our behalf so that we can have a relationship with Him, and that's because He wants it! Not us. No wonder so many of those who trusted in Him in the New Testament stuck around. The New Testament gospel made much of Jesus, not much of man. It's not that there weren't any false professions in New Testament times. It just seems that the majority of professions, if the Book of Acts tells even half of the story, were genuine, and produced fruit. I don't mean that people exhibited the outward signs that we often look for. I mean there was at least a desire to know Jesus more, and to become better acquainted with Him. Acts 2 is a wonderful example of this. Peter preaches what is likely the most powerful gospel message recorded in the New Testament. The message climaxes in the powerful declaration, "Therefore let all the house of Israel know assuredly, that God hath made that same Jesus, whom ye have crucified, both Lord and Christ (Acts 2:36)." Peter tells them what they must do, and this is the result, "they that gladly received his word were baptized: and the same day there were added unto them about three thousand souls. And they continued stedfastly in the apostles' doctrine and fellowship, and in breaking of bread, and in prayers (Acts 2:41-42)."

- Here are the results of genuine faith following a gospel that centered on Jesus instead of man.
  - o Those that received his word were baptized.
  - o They all continued steadfastly in the apostle's doctrine and fellowship.

NOTE: I know how we like to use the word 'fellowship,' but to quote one of the classics, "you keep using that word. I do not think it means what you think it means."[28] When we think of a fellowship, we think of a time to get together and hang out. There is usually food involved. That isn't entirely off, but there is more to the biblical concept of fellowship than just getting together. It means, "a having in common (koinos), partnership..."[29] If we're not careful, our fellowships really are nothing more than just get togethers. What Luke describes in Acts 2 is a very real sense of community that these new believers continued in that centered upon one commonality and that is their mutual faith in Jesus as the Christ. That was the unifying factor that caused them to be together. It caused them to learn together. It caused them to grow together. It caused them to work together. It caused them to suffer and sacrifice together. This is the biblical idea of true fellowship and it is a wonderful product of genuine faith in Jesus! John records Jesus saying plainly, "By this shall all men know that ye are my disciples, if ye have love one to another." A biblical gospel produces real fellowship in genuine believers. A commonality with common goals, etc.

o They also fellowshipped as we define it today – they ate together from house to house.

NOTE: I have done quite a bit of research on this idea of breaking bread from house to house and many scholars are divided as to what idea is being presented here. Some believe this is a reference to the Lord's Supper. Others believe this is merely a matter of spending time together around food. I am inclined to believe this is a reference to the real sense of community among believers. They loved one another and loved being together. This new community was their family. Remember what Jesus said to those who told Him that his mom and brothers were looking for Him?

"Then one said unto him, Behold, thy mother and thy brethren stand without, desiring to speak with thee. But he answered and said unto him that told him, Who is my mother? and who are my brethren? And he stretched forth his hand toward his disciples, and said, Behold my mother and my brethren! For whosoever shall do the will of my Father which is in heaven, the same is my brother, and sister, and mother." Matthew 12:47-50

One of the main reasons I am inclined to think getting together around food is in view here is because many of the Jewish commentators hold this view. It seems sensible to me that they are inclined to have the best sense regarding their own culture, which the Jerusalem church was still very much inundated with Jewish culture. Especially at this point when we are reading of a group of people that were freshly won out of Judaism to Christ.

So, they learned together, had a real sense of commonality, fellowshipped together, and...

    o   They prayed together.

They continued steadfastly, or unwaveringly in these areas. I am just trying to point out that while they may not have looked much different the day after they trusted Christ than they did the day before, there was still something very different in them. The day before they were indifferent to Jesus, and the day of and apparently long after, they were very interested in knowing Him more.

Genuine faith in a biblical gospel that makes much of Jesus rather than man creates disciples!

So, with that in mind, what is the gospel?

- The gospel is first and foremost all about who Jesus is!
  - o Let's look at a few of the gospel messages recorded for us in Scripture.
    - ■ In Luke 2:10-11, the angel says, "Fear not: for, behold, I bring you good tidings of great joy, which shall be to all people. For unto you is born this day in the city of David a Saviour, which is Christ the Lord."
      - First, I want to point out that "good tidings" is the same Greek word that is translated "gospel" in other passages.
      - So, here we have the gospel being preached by an angel on the day of Jesus' birth.

- What is it all about – a Saviour, the Christ, has been born unto you this day in the city of David.
  - We already looked at Acts 2:36, but again, what was that message all about – Jesus, and specifically who Jesus is!
  - Paul's manner, as Luke refers to it, was to open and allege, "that Christ must needs have suffered, and risen again from the dead; and that this Jesus, whom I preach unto you, is Christ (Acts 17:3)."
  - o So, the gospel is all about Jesus, and primarily who He is, but that's not all.

- This last passage in Acts 17, helps us see that the gospel is also about why Jesus came!
  - o Paul's manner was to help people see that Christ needed to suffer and rise again.
  - o Now obviously this is Luke's summary of the subject matter of Paul's preaching, but the point of Paul's preaching was to help people see who Jesus is and why He came.

NOTE: You have to remember that Luke is speaking primarily of Paul's efforts in synagogues with Jewish people. One of their primary objections to Jesus' identity as the Messiah was the fact that He suffered and died. So, Paul's effort to help them see that it was necessary for the Christ to have suffered and risen again was definitely part of helping them accept that Jesus is the Messiah, but in the process of helping them see why it was necessary that Christ suffer and rise again, he was helping them see why Jesus, the Messiah, came in the first place.

- o Paul would write to Timothy, "This is a faithful saying, and worthy of all acceptation, that Christ Jesus came into the world to save sinners; of whom I am chief."
- o One of my favorite passages in all of Scripture is John 3:17 where Jesus says, "For God sent not his Son into the world to condemn the world; but that the world through him might be saved."
- o The angel tells Joseph in a dream, "And she shall bring forth a son, and thou shalt call his name JESUS: for he shall save his people from their sins (Matthew 1:21)."

What is the gospel? It's the good news that a Savior has come, and that Savior is Jesus! It's the good news of who Jesus is and why He came! It's all about Him!

- • A biblical gospel also explains how He did what He came to do, and why it was necessary – "Opening and alleging, that Christ <u>must needs</u> have suffered, and risen again from the dead…"
- o What Jesus came to do was necessary.
- o No one explains this better than Paul
- o In Romans 3, Paul addresses man's effort to establish his own righteousness while also showing man's need for Christ's righteousness.
  - ■ V.19 – the purpose of the law is to clearly and effectively establish the guilt of us all.

- V.22-23 – we are all in the same boat as transgressors of God's law – aka sinners.
- V.24-26 – justification and redemption are available through Jesus because He is God's propitiation on our behalf!

NOTE: Propitiation means that which makes things right. It has the idea of making amends or satisfying or making things right. Jesus is God's way of making things right between us and Him! Consider something that Timothy Keller included in his book on preaching. It's lengthy, but so good:

"Ray Dillard, one of the authors of An Introduction to the Old Testament, once told me personally that one of the main questions constantly raised by the historical books, from Judges through 2 Chronicles, has to do with the nature of the covenant. The covenant is "I will take you as my own people, and I will be your God" (Exodus 6:7). The question is this: In light of the constant failures of the people to live up to their covenant promises to serve God, is the covenant conditional or unconditional? ("Because you broke the covenant, I will cut you off, curse you, and abandon you forever.") Or will he say it is unconditional? ("Though you have rejected me, I will never wholly abandon you, but I will remain with you.") Which is it? Ray said that anyone reading the Old Testament closely will find that sometimes God seems to be saying it is conditional, while other times he seems to be assuring the people that it is unconditional. This mystery is one of the main tensions that drive the dramatic action. Since his people have forsaken him, will he forsake them?

There seems to be no simple answer that will not compromise something we know of God. Will his holiness give way to his love, so that he overlooks sin? Or will his love be overwhelmed by his holiness and justice, so that the divine hammer falls? Either way it seems he is not as truly loving or as truly holy as he otherwise reveals himself to be. See the plot tension in the story?

And then Jesus comes, and as we see him crying, "My God, my God, why have you forsaken me?" we realize the answer. Is the covenant between God and his people conditional or unconditional? Yes. Yes. Jesus came and fulfilled the conditions so God could love us unconditionally."[30]

- o Paul writes in his second letter to the Corinthians that, "he [God] hath made him [Jesus] to be sin for us, who knew no sin; that we might be made the righteousness of God in him (2 Corinthians 5:21)."
  - We all sin.
  - This sin separates us from God.
  - Something has to be done with the sin in order for us to have a relationship with Him.
  - In walks Jesus.
  - Jesus took that sin on Himself, paid for it in our place satisfying the wrath of God for us, and in its place offers His righteousness so that God sees us as He sees Jesus!
- o That is what Jesus' death on the cross accomplished.

- So, the gospel is all about who Jesus is and why He came, but what does a person do with that?

o   I think this is a natural response to the gospel being presented.

o   When a person gets it, and they believe it, it is natural for them to want to know what to do with it.

o   We see this on more than one occasion in the Bible.

- Saul asked something along these lines at his conversion in Acts 9.

- The Jewish people Peter preached to in Acts 2 asked a similar question.

- The Philippian jailer also asked in Acts 16.

- Even the Ethiopian eunuch's question was along these lines in Acts 8.

o   The answer is simple, but we struggle with it sometimes.

- The answer is "put your faith in Jesus," and it carries with it the idea of understanding what you've just heard regarding Him – who He is and what He did – and believing it; putting your trust in His work on the cross instead of your own work here on earth, or anything else.

- This is the plain truth all throughout Scripture.

  - In Ephesians 2:8-9, Paul says that we are saved by grace through faith.

  - In Romans 3, over and over Paul says that we are justified or redeemed through faith in Jesus or by believing in Jesus.

  - In Romans 10, Paul gives us sort of an outline in v.14 by asking a series of questions: "How then shall they call on him in whom they have not believed? and how shall they believe in him of whom they have not heard? and how shall they hear without a preacher?"

NOTE: Romans 10:14 sort of begs a question. Does a person need to pray a prayer in order to be saved? Based on Scripture, my opinion is no. It's about appropriated trust or faith. This is the witness throughout Scripture. This can certainly manifest itself in a verbal request for salvation, but it may not always. Earlier in the same chapter Paul uses the term confess. This is more like what we see in Acts 8 with the Ethiopian eunuch. We like seeing people pray a prayer because it gives us a sense of peace about the whole thing. It's a tangible way to 'see it happen.' It's like confirmation for us, but with Philip in Acts 8, the eunuch's confession was enough for him.

Just remember that a person can pray a prayer and never truly appreciate who Jesus is or what He has done and thus never actually begin to trust in His work on the cross. A person can however; hear, understand, believe, and trust, and never prayer the sinner's prayer and Jesus will save them because of their faith.

This is the gospel, and it's all about Him! It makes sense that, because it totally revolves around who Jesus is, people who truly trust in Him as a result would also be inclined to follow Him.

Now, I know that when it is looked at this way, it can seem like a complex and long process. It doesn't have to be, but neither is it bad if it is (long and drawn out I mean). It never needs to be complex when presented. Obviously, the purpose behind the detail here is to carry the point.

Summary:

So, what is the Gospel?

It's good news! It is irrefutable proof that God loves you. He loves *you*! He loves you, right now, just the way you are!

God loves us and wants us to be in fellowship with Him. He wants to have a relationship with us, but in order for that to be possible, something had to be done about the sin that separates us from Him. God is love, and God is mercy, but God is also holy, and God is just. He couldn't simply overlook sin. Justice demands payment. Jesus steps in to satisfy it all! The requirements of God's holiness and justice are satisfied in Jesus on the cross. Sin was paid for in full. What love! What wisdom! What mercy! I can't remember where I read this, but it isn't original with me – *God treated Jesus like we deserve so that He can treat us like Jesus deserves.*

The gracious and merciful God of creation sent His Son, Jesus, to rescue those He loves from their sin so they can have a relationship with Him! Jesus, the pure and perfect, sinless Son of God took your sin and my sin, and the sins of the world upon Himself and suffered and died on our behalf so that God could know us, and so that we could know God. He wants to know you! He wants you to know Him, and He loved you enough to make a way where there was no way.

That's who Jesus is! That's why Jesus came! Do you believe? Will you stop looking to everything else or anything else and put your trust in Him?

That is the gospel. That is good news!

There are a million ways to word it, and there are a million aspects to emphasize about it based on the context within which you are witnessing.

Another very important point regarding the gospel that I'd like to consider with you is the mindset that just because you don't have the passages in Scripture memorized therefore you don't know or can't effectively preach or present the gospel.

This simply isn't true.

Please understand that the gospel can be supported by and explained with Scripture, ***but it is based on an event in history that is true and powerful on its own*** and predates any New Testament Scripture by almost ***twenty*** years. I say that because, though I believe it's best to use and explain Scripture to preach the gospel, the gospel is a thing all on its own that people declared for a long time before any New Testament Scripture was available. You can preach the gospel without memorizing or taking anyone to even one passage of Scripture. Again, people did that for quite some time while the New Testament was being completed.

You may not fully understand the ***doctrine***, or all of the ***theology***. You may not be able to quote or show people all the various verses, <u>but that doesn't mean you can't preach the gospel.</u>

Finally, before we conclude…

I want to address the tendency to rush people straight to the gospel.

I know that Scripture makes it clear that we aren't promised another second, and we want to be blameless. I understand, but we also need to want to do more than make sure people's blood isn't on our hands. We, hopefully, truly desire to see people reached. If you have an open door and perhaps something conversationally has lent itself to broaching the gospel directly, then great, but if not, there has to be room for at least an element of 'come and see' in our efforts.

There is biblical precedent for this.

In John 1:37-51, both Peter and Nathanael were won this way. They were invited to come and see Jesus for themselves.

In John 4:27-30 the woman at the well, convinced that she has met the Messiah, runs back to the village and says, 'come and see ...' In vv. 39-42, many believed because of what she said and many more believed because of seeing Him with their own eyes and hearing Him for themselves.

Jesus is absolutely still at work today! He is at work in the lives of individuals and in the lives of churches, and there is nothing wrong with inviting a lost or unchurched person to come, either into your life or into your church or into the lives of other believers that you know, so that they can witness that work firsthand. That doesn't mean you can't discuss the gospel beforehand, but if that opportunity isn't there, or even if it doesn't get very far, don't be afraid to invite them into your life, the life of your church, or to some church activity with other believers, so that they may "…taste and see that the Lord is good: blessed is the man that trusteth in Him. (Psalm 34:8)"

"But sanctify the Lord God in your hearts: and be ready always to give an answer to every man that asketh you a reason of the hope that is in you with meekness and fear: (1 Peter 3:15)"

Conclusion:

Paul's boldness came from having a right perspective and great faith regarding the gospel of Christ and the God of that gospel! He understood himself to be a debtor. He was deeply obligated to this work of preaching the gospel to everyone, everywhere, but it was a genuine burden and not just a duty. Paul wasn't concerned about numbers for the sake of feeling validated in his calling. He cared for lost souls, understood that the majority of mankind was lost and without hope, and was thus compelled, having himself benefitted unworthily from the power of the gospel of Jesus Christ, to take that gospel to all. "For though I preach the gospel, I have nothing to glory of: for necessity is laid upon me; yea, woe is unto me, if I preach not the gospel!" (1 Cor. 9:16). Paul cared for the lost for Christ's sake and the sake of the lost. He was a ***debtor***.

He also had ***great faith*** in the ***power*** of the gospel. Paul believed the gospel wasn't just a clever argument by which he might win people to God. It was the power of God. The gospel, for Paul, was supernatural. It, along with the Holy Spirit of God, could work beyond what Paul could see. He knew this all too well, for after he had walked away from the gospel himself as Saul of Tarsus – the persecutor of Jesus' followers, the truth of that message continued to "prick" his heart (Acts 9:5b). The gospel is powerful, carrying with it the power of God. It can convict (ask Paul), and it can save.

So, because of Paul's perspective and his faith—he believed the gospel had power—he was bold. He wasn't arrogant, ***obnoxious***, ***haughty***, or ***belligerent***. He was confident in the power of God and so he wasn't timid. He was bold. He was ready. He wasn't ashamed but preached the gospel every chance he got.

What is your perspective? Do you consider yourself a debtor to others regarding the gospel? Do you have faith in the power of the gospel? Do you see the gospel as sufficient to convict and convince the mind of _____ (insert the name of a family member, coworker, neighbor, or lost friend in the blank) and to save his/her soul? I would meditate on those thoughts and consider them before the Lord for a bit.

If you are saved, you are a debtor. You have a real obligation to others that are where you were and need to be where you are. The gospel is powerful beyond what we can see. It is sufficient. It can do the work you and I can't. God is able to convince and convict through His Word and His Spirit. Trust Him and trust the power of His gospel. That's where our boldness and confidence need to come from. Our confidence needs to be in God, not in our own abilities.

Paul had great boldness. He had the boldness that is often lacking in Christianity today. We need it. We need to get it back, but it will only come as our perspective changes and our faith grows.

WITNESSING LIKE PAUL: SECTION 4

Paul Was Contextually Sensitive in His Effort to Lead Others to Jesus!

—ɷ—

Section Aim

The purpose of section four is to demonstrate the importance of trying to ***identify where people are*** spiritually before trying to give them the information necessary to get them where they need to be.

Paul Was Contextually Sensitive in His Effort to Lead Others to Jesus!

"And Paul said, 'I would to God, that not only thou, but also all that hear me this day, were both almost, and altogether such as I am, except these bonds.'"
The Apostle Paul

Paul knew how to use a *map* . . .

Or at least he understood the keys to using a map.

Well good. I'm glad that is so. What does that have to do with Paul's approach to witnessing? Everything!

- In order for a map to be of any use, there are certain things you need to know.
  o First, you need to know *where you are going*, but that information alone isn't enough.
  o You also need to know *where you are*.
  o Until you have identified both places on the map, it is useless.
  o Once you have identified both places on the map, you can effectively use the map to chart a course from where you are to where you want to go.

- Perhaps for our generation the Maps app on your phone would be a better illustration.
  o The same principle applies.
  o There are two fields that you have to fill in, in order for the app to do what it does: "To" and "From".
  o Without that information, the app is useless.

That's great, but I still don't understand what that has to do with Paul's approach to witnessing. Well, it begins to make sense when you consider what Paul was trying to ***accomplish***.

Paul was trying to reconcile people to God.

- Reconciling man to God represents the "To" field in your Maps app, or the destination on a map.

In 2 Corinthians 5:18–21, Paul writes:

> And all things *are* of God, who hath ***reconciled us to himself*** by Jesus Christ, and hath given to us the ministry of reconciliation; to wit, that ***God was*** in Christ, ***reconciling the world unto himself***, not imputing their trespasses unto them; and hath committed unto us the word of reconciliation. Now then we are ambassadors for Christ, as though God did beseech *you* by us: we pray *you* in Christ's stead, ***be ye reconciled to God***. For he hath made him *to be* sin for us, who knew no sin; that we might be made the righteousness of God in him.

- The word "reconcile" means to ***change*** or ***exchange***.[31]
  - o One example given is that of exchanging coins for that of equivalent value.[32]
  - o The way the word is used here, Paul packages not only what God did, but what He accomplished by it, together.
  - o God exchanged Jesus for us (v.21); Jesus took our place.

o As we talked about in the last section, the Bible word is "propitiation" (Romans 3:25; 1 John 2:2, 4:10).

o The word "propitiation" has to do with expiation, which is a fancy word that means "making an atonement."[33]

o It's "the means whereby sin is covered and remitted" or cancelled, making it possible for man and God to come together.[34]

o God provided a way to eliminate the very thing that keeps man from Him through Jesus.

o He has provided a means of reconciliation, and Paul is interested in and trying to reconcile man to God.

• The effort of reconciling people to God is the work of getting them from ***one place*** spiritually and mentally ***to another***; it's like taking them on a ***spiritual journey***.

He was trying to get them from Point A, where they were, to Point B, which is where God is.

• Now, while Point B—where God is, was/is ***static***, Point A, where people were/are ***spiritually***, wasn't/isn't.

o People, depending on their upbringing, life experiences, religious background, and cultural context, were and are all over the place.

o In order to effectively get people to Point B, Paul has to first determine where they are ***spiritually***.

o In other words, he needs to accurately determine where Point A is for each person or group of people.

So, does that mean in order to witness effectively, Paul had to know everything about every religion under heaven, or about every person he would try to reach? **No**. Paul, it seems, based on his preaching, tried to answer one question: Where were they regarding God? That seemed to influence Paul's route with the gospel most. And certainly, the more you know, the better, but knowing everything there is to know is impossible and unnecessary. However, Point A, where they were spiritually or where they were regarding God, was and is important, and so . . .

Paul's message would be different based on an audience's Point A (whether it was a person or a group of people).

NOTE: Now, just to clarify, everyone is born dead in trespasses and in sins. Every person is born spiritually dead, separated from the Father. That is universal. That is not what I am referring to as "Point A" on the map. Again, I think from Paul's preaching we can conclude that where a person is regarding God and the existence of God is key to being able to help them understand even this element of sin and sin nature.

Remember also, that we do not have a record of the content of every message preached by the apostle Paul, but in that which has been supplied, there is a difference in content based his audience.

Questions such as: Does this person already believe in Jehovah, does this person believe in a different god or gods, do they put any stock in the Bible (basically the Old Testament in Paul's day), do they believe in any deity or do they claim to be atheist, etc. would have, and did have a bearing on Paul's efforts to help them understand who Jesus is and why He came.

Even a basic understanding of one's culture can do much to help guide their efforts with the gospel as we'll see.

- When Paul preached to the Jews, he went straight to the ***identity of Jesus***, working to prove that Jesus is the Christ through their Scriptures (Old Testament).
  o Acts 9:20–22:

And ***straightway he preached Christ in the synagogues***, that he is the Son of God. But all that heard him were amazed, and said; "Is not this he that destroyed them which called on this name in Jerusalem, and came hither for that intent, that he might bring them bound unto the chief priests?" But Saul increased the more in strength, and confounded the Jews which dwelt at Damascus, ***proving that this is very Christ.***

  o Acts 13:14–52, *v.23, 33: "Of this man's seed hath God according to his promise raised unto Israel a Saviour, Jesus. … God hath fulfilled the same unto us their children, in that he hath raised up Jesus again; as it is also written in the second psalm, 'Thou art my Son, this day have I begotten thee.'"
  o Acts 17:1–3:

Now when they had passed through Amphipolis and Apollonia, they came to Thessalonica, where was a synagogue of the Jews: And Paul, as his manner was, went in unto them, and three sabbath days reasoned with them out of the scriptures, Opening and alleging, that ***Christ must***

needs have suffered, and risen again from the dead; and that this Jesus, whom I preach unto you, is Christ.

- o Acts 22:1-22: here, in Paul's testimony, he connects Jesus to "***that Just One***" in v.14 while working toward the gospel.
    - ▪ His audience was Jewish, which is crystal clear from the context.
    - ▪ His reference to the Just One would have made no sense to a Gentile.
    - ▪ He made the reference specifically because of who he was speaking to.

So, you see a clear pattern in his effort to reconcile Jewish people to God. His effort was to help them see and embrace who Jesus is. They already knew God. They needed to know Jesus. So, he jumped right to that point.

- • When Paul preached to Gentiles, which were typically pagan (polytheistic), he began by making a case for God as the creator of all things.
    - o Acts 14:15: "And saying, 'Sirs, why do ye these things? We also are men of like passions with you, and preach unto you that ***ye should turn*** from these vanities ***unto the living God***, which made heaven, and earth, and the sea, and all things that are therein. . .'"
    - o Acts 17:16–32: Paul, while preaching to the philosophers of Athens said:

As I passed by, and beheld your devotions, I found an altar with this inscription, TO THE UNKNOWN GOD. Whom therefore ye ignorantly worship, him declare I unto you. ___God that made the world and all things therein,___ seeing that he is Lord of heaven and earth, dwelleth not in temples made with hands; Neither is worshipped with men's hands, as though he needed any thing, seeing he giveth to all life, and breath, and all things… (vv.23-25, emphasis mine)

- o Again, in the same chapter (Acts 17), it is clear that Paul also preached about Jesus and the resurrection, but we can see here, in vv.23-25, as he began to preach to a new audience of Greeks, where he began with the God of creation.

- • One other ___example___ of Paul's consideration for the spiritual and even cultural context of his audience, or their Point A, and ___evidence___ of the effects it has, is in his attempt to witness to King Agrippa in Acts 26:1–28.

Wait a minute. Festus and Agrippa were representatives of the Roman government. Paul is preaching to them the same way he preached to the Jews. Doesn't that contradict your entire argument? Not really. There is a reason Paul used the same approach here as he would have done before a Jewish audience.

- o Agrippa, the one Paul was addressing, was a ___Jew___.

"He was conversant with all the Jewish laws and customs, and a firm believer in the prophetic writings."[35]

The arguments of Paul had been so rational; the appeal which he had made to his belief of the prophets had been so irresistible, that he had been nearly convinced of the truth of Christianity. We are to remember ... That Agrippa was a Jew, and that he would look on this whole subject in a different manner from the Roman Festus.[36]

> o   Notice in v.24 that, while Agrippa understood perfectly what Paul was trying to do, Festus had ___no appreciation___ whatsoever for Paul's approach with the gospel here: "And as he thus spake for himself, Festus said with a loud voice, 'Paul, thou art beside thyself; much learning doth make thee mad.'"

"Paul had deliberately been using language which while intelligible to Agrippa the Jew, to whom the defense is chiefly directed, might well appear to the sophisticated Roman as the ravings of a demented apocalyptist!"[37]

NOTE: By the way, this is the second account of Paul using his ___testimony___ to present the gospel as well. I think it is worth noting that both times were in an effort to reach Jewish people. Paul is empathizing with those he is reaching out to, letting them know he understands where they are coming from. I think this is a powerful tool when it is genuinely available!

So, there is an obvious difference in Paul's approach with the gospel based on who he was talking to, and I think, practically speaking, the reasoning is fairly straightforward. Here is the reality:

Paul knew all needed to be saved, and salvation is the same for all, but not all were in the same place regarding their ability to appreciate that need, and so he _adjusted his approach_ to the gospel accordingly.

- Point A was not the same for both groups.
  - o Paul understood the Jews believed in God but misunderstood how to be reconciled to Him.
  - o Paul also understood the Gentiles (for the most part) were not convinced of or always aware that there was a God to which one needed to be reconciled.

- Because Point A could not be the same for both groups, the route to Point B, reconciliation with God through the gospel, couldn't be either.

- And so, because he identified the Point A of each group, he was able, to the best of his ability, to chart a suitable course to Point B for each group.

One final thought:

I think this is a natural thing for anyone who truly desires to effectively <u>communicate the gospel</u>.

Paul's regard for the spiritual and religious context of those he reached out to, and his desire to actually reach them, is precisely what compelled him to <u>customize</u> his approach!

NOTE: This isn't unique to Paul. Jesus practiced this as well as Peter, Stephen, and Philip. It may be a matter of common sense.

- I think it simply stemmed naturally from a genuine desire to ***communicate truth***.
  - o There is a difference between making a lot of information available to someone to take or leave at their discretion and trying to communicate with them regarding a matter.
  - o For instance, consider the work of any good preacher or teacher.
    - ■ A good preacher or teacher isn't simply dumping information on you.
    - ■ They have a point they are trying to get across; something they are trying to communicate, and they will not be satisfied until you get it.
    - ■ While they are teaching, they are looking for cues either visually or audibly, or they are asking questions, and the purpose is to see if you are indeed getting it.
    - ■ If it is clear that you aren't getting it, they will try a different approach, or maybe try to illustrate the point in some other way.
    - ■ The point is they aren't interested in simply dumping information on you.

- Paul wasn't looking to dump information on people.
  - o He was interested in communicating with them.
  - o He was interested in them getting it and being able to make an informed decision as a result.
  - o That is the cause for the exchange between Agrippa and Paul in Acts 26:27–29:

King Agrippa, believest thou the prophets? *I know that thou believest*. *Then Agrippa said unto Paul,* "Almost thou **persuadest** me to be a Christian." *And Paul said,* "I would to God, that not only thou, but also all that hear me this day, were both **_almost_**, and **_altogether_** such as I am, except these bonds."

- Consider that children, some of the best untrained debaters/negotiators on the planet, are good at making their case and are persistent, not because they read a book on negotiating and sales, but because they genuinely want what they are after, and so they figure out a way.

- Paul's **_desire_** to communicate truth and reach people, I believe, caused him to be careful in regarding, as much as possible, the spiritual and religious context of those he was speaking to because he knew sensitivity in this way was the best chance of them **_trusting Jesus_**, and really, it just makes good sense.

By the way:

   o Context is "the situation in which something happens: the group of conditions that exist where and when something happens."[38]
   o Conditions are "attendant circumstances."[39]

- Consider once again Paul's purpose for preaching, according to 2 Corinthians 5:18-21.
   o It is to reconcile man to God.

> o In order to do that, Paul has to get a person to look to **_Jesus_**.

- Now consider Paul's logic in Romans 10:13–14.
  - o In order for a person to call on Jesus (look to Him as the only means of salvation), they must first **_believe_**.
  - o In order for them to believe, they must **_hear_**.
  - o In order for them to hear, there must be a **_preacher_** (not in the official sense, but someone preaching/proclaiming the gospel, someone witnessing of Him).

- Now consider that in order for a person to look to Jesus for salvation, they must not only believe that He is able to help, but that they need help.
  - o This was the problem of both the Jew and the Gentile.
  - o Neither understood their need for help.
  - o The Jews knew God, but not their need for atonement, trusting in their own sacrifices, which were merely a picture of what the Messiah would be.
  - o The Gentiles knew neither and thus had no sense of having offended God by virtue of having had no sense of the One True God to begin with.

So. . .

> o In order to get people from either group to a point where they understood, not only that Jesus is the Messiah, but that they even needed Him as Savior, Paul's work in identifying their Point A was essential.

71

o Without it he wouldn't know what the primary obstacle to them seeing their need was.

o Thus, he couldn't begin to try to overcome it.

If they don't see their need for the *__journey__*, they aren't going to take it.

NOTE: We want to be careful here. It is essential that people understand their need, but here is where we can be tempted to make this all about them instead of all about Him! We can try to "sell" them salvation and use what the Bible says about their situation as a way to scare them into Jesus' arms. The problem is, they aren't going to Him because of who He is. They are going to Him to save their own necks. Their need and instinct for self-preservation is running the show. Jesus becomes nothing more than "fire insurance." This is not okay, and it's somewhat dishonest, especially when we make so "easy." Just pray and, basically, all your troubles in this sense will go away. Is salvation simple? Yes. Is it straight forward? Yes. But only real faith in the person and work of Jesus will do. <u>This is a faith that can be followed by or accompanied with and inclines a person to respond to a call to follow as well.</u> Jesus isn't interested in being used. He is who He is. We need Him, but He is worthy of following even if becoming His disciple never netted us one ounce of Heaven! We aren't preaching a works-based salvation, but we need to be preaching a God and Jesus centered gospel. People need to understand their need for Him, but be careful not to make the gospel all about them. I am trying to be clear here, and I hope this is coming across right, but I have heard too many "gospel messages" that are consumed with sin and hell and say very little about God and Jesus. Sin and hell are part of it, but only so much as to help people understand why Jesus came in the first place.

So, with that in mind, let's go ahead and wrap this section up…

Conclusion:

Again, it's like using a map. Knowing where you want to go isn't enough. It is equally important that you know ***where you are***.

Paul understood this and thus reached out to people accordingly. That doesn't mean that you have to wait years to witness to a person. You don't have to fully understand everything about them on a personal level. You should get to know them on a personal level. You should grow to know them and love them, but you don't have to know every personal detail before you try to witness. Follow the leadership of the Holy Spirit, but always try and get a feel for where a person is spiritually so that, when the opportunity does present itself, you can give them the best opportunity possible to ***trust in Jesus***!

By the way, the more you know about a person, the more opportunities you will see, and the more onramps to the gospel you will find.

Recommended Resources on this Topic:

- *The Unchurched Next Door* by Thom Rainer
- *The Millennials* by Thom Rainer
- *Inside the Mind of Unchurched Harry and Mary* by Lee Strobel

WITNESSING LIKE PAUL: SECTION 5

Reasoning, Disputing, Persuading, and Testifying

—⟋ϻ⟍—

Section Aim

The purpose of section five is to help Christians see the many ways in which Paul worked to help people understand and trust in who Jesus is and what He did for them.

Reasoning, Disputing, Persuading, and Testifying

"And Paul said, 'I would to God, that not only thou, but also all that hear me this day, were both almost, and altogether such as I am, except these bonds.'"
The Apostle Paul

I'm a lover, not a *fighter*...

You may be turned off by the title of this section in the series. The thought of **_confrontation_** may seem **_intimidating_** to you. You may be inclined to inform me that you are a lover, not a fighter. Let me tell you, though, that if you are not willing to be a fighter, you can't claim to be much of a lover because the Bible paints a bleak picture for those who refuse to trust in Jesus and His work on the cross.

- All have **_sinned_** (Romans 3:10).
  - o We all suffer from a corrupt nature: a nature that is separated from God as a result of Adam and Eve's sin in the garden (Genesis 5:1–3, Ephesians 2:1–3).
  - o That doesn't mean that we are all as wicked as we could possibly be.
  - o It simply means that we are all inclined to go our own way.
  - o Consider that we have to teach children right, but not wrong.
  - o Wrong comes naturally.

- The wages of sin is ***death***.
  - o Physical death is a result of Adam and Eve's sin in the garden, as is the existence of our sin nature — our natural ***propensity*** to sin (Genesis 2:16–17; 3:19; 5:1–3, Romans 5:19a, Hebrews 9:27a).
  - o Because of sin, we are born ***spiritually*** dead, or separated from the Father.
  - o If we die physically, spiritually dead (separated from the Father because of sin), we will be spiritually dead (separated from the Father) for all ***eternity***, first in hell and then in the Lake of Fire (Romans 6:23a, Rev. 20:13–14; 21:8).

- The ***only way*** to avoid eternal separation from God in the Lake of Fire is to be reconciled to God by ***grace*** through ***faith*** before we die physically (Romans 6:23; 10:13, Ephesians 2:8–9).
  - o Grace is getting what you don't deserve: God's favor.
  - o Faith is believing and receiving the truth of the gospel.
  - o You must believe in the ***identity*** of Jesus as the Christ, the Son of the living God, and thus that His sacrifice on the cross was ***sufficient*** to pay the price for your sins.
  - o This is evidenced by His resurrection from the dead, and believing you must put your trust in Him, making you His disciple (Acts 2:36–38; 8:36–37, Romans 3:20-28, 1 John 2:2; 4:10; 5:11–12).

- There is absolutely no other way for a person to be **_reconciled to God_**; it is through faith in Christ and Christ alone.

Acts 4:12: "Neither is there salvation in any other: for there is none other name under heaven given among men, whereby we must be saved."

So, understand that unless people set aside their thinking, whatever it is, and accept that Jesus is who He says He is and that His work on the cross is the way to be reconciled with the Father (and thus the only way to have a home in heaven), then there is absolutely no hope for them.

How are they going to know unless you are **_willing_** to tell them?

- Now, the problem isn't that people simply **_don't know_**, and thus don't **_believe_**.
  - o There are many that don't know and thus don't believe, but there are others, many others, that believe **_something else_** entirely.
  - o They already have established thinking on the matter of heaven and hell, eternity, right and wrong, good and evil, and who and what is and isn't deity.
  - o The good news is that God is okay with different thoughts and different views so long as we are all good people. . . Right?
  - o All roads lead to heaven. Right?
  - o Of course, not. . .

- So, if people are to have any hope, God's people—those that are armed with the gospel—are going to have to be willing to tell them, and that is going to require some confrontation.

Now, one final thing before we get going.

- There is a difference between _**contending**_ and being _**contentious**_.

This is not a televised debate. No one is keeping score. We want to share the truth with people because God loves them and wants to have a relationship with them and sent Jesus to die for them to make that possible. This is not the same as arguing. This is not the same as fighting. This isn't about winning. If they are not receptive, or if they are combative, then you need to simply back away and wait for another _**opportunity**_. If, however, they are willing to "reason" with you, and allow you to "reason" with them, then you have a green light and a golden opportunity to be a witness. So, if you mean what you say, and you are indeed a lover, not a fighter, then you ought to make a great witness!

Back to the map. . .

- In the last section, we compared Paul's approach to witnessing with charting a _**course**_ on a map.

- In order to chart a course on a map, you need to identify two things.
  - o You need to know ***where you are***, and you need to know ***where you are trying to go***.
  - o Once those two points are clearly established, the course can be determined, and the journey can begin.

- This is the way Paul handled the gospel.
  - o Having already determined where he wanted to take people, he then had to determine where people were, ***spiritually***.
    - Were they pagan, polytheists who needed first to be introduced to the God of creation?
    - Were they Jewish monotheists who did not believe Jesus was the Christ because they did not understand the prophecies of their own Scriptures?
    - Or were they something else entirely?
  - o Once he identified a person's Point A, he could then work to get them to Point B.

So, the points are: Point A: ***where they are*** spiritually; Point B: being reconciled to God. An important part of the journey is helping them sense their need.

- It is important to understand that much of this is ***pre-work***.
  - o You need to have a sense of how you are going to get them to point B before you really start trying to lead them there.

o   This is merely a matter of charting the proper or best course to take.

o   It's not until all of this is done that the work of moving someone or leading someone down the determined path begins.

o   Even once you get started, you still need to be flexible and ready to alter course if necessary.

• Hopefully, seeing Paul's consideration for personal context in his effort to witness helps you see the advantages in focusing on and stewarding properly those within your immediate sphere of influence such as coworkers, neighbors, friends, and family.

o   You already know them or at least have a reason to know them, and so, striking up a conversation doesn't have to be awkward.

o   The more rapport you have with someone, the more likely they are to discuss some of the more touchy or controversial issues of life.

o   On top of that, your testimony before this person over an extended period of time should bolster your credibility, and the credibility of the gospel.

NOTE: I want to be careful here not to give you the wrong impression. When I say your testimony should bolster your credibility and the credibility of the gospel, I don't mean that you have to have behaved like a saint around them. Many people are afraid to witness because they know that those closest to them are aware of their flaws and weaknesses. Your weaknesses are the brightest billboard or backdrop for the grace of God through Christ. Paul said he would glory in his infirmities.

The point isn't to glory in sin, but in the grace and goodness of Christ that is greater than our weaknesses! Yes, you are a sinner, but nothing can separate you from the love of Christ. You may get it wrong sometimes, but Jesus is still with you and as long as you are trying to walk with Him, He is still working on you (Romans 8:28-29)!

In addition…

o   Your proximity should help you get the clearest picture of where a person is spiritually and philosophically.

o   They trust you and know that you care for them and your interest in them goes further than your efforts to convert them.

o   They know your love and interest in them isn't contingent upon their reception of your witness (this is huge).

So, get to know those around you. Reach out to them. Try to spend time with them. Love them. Don't just do nice things for them. Consider that ***sacrifice*** is generally associated with love and love them. Give up time, effort, energy, and money, if it is necessary.

The ***more*** this becomes a regular part of your life, the ***more*** witnessing ***opportunities*** you will have!

My observation is that our reluctance to focus on reaching those God has brought into our immediate sphere of influence is the associated risk. Someone said to me once, "You can't lose what you never had." There point was something else entirely, but in this regard, they are right on. I think we are more okay with witnessing to people we don't know because there is less potential cost involved. If they don't like me as a result, it's not as big of a deal because I'll likely not see them again anyway. But if I witness to those that I see every day or that I live next door to or that I am related to and it doesn't go well... You see what I mean? However, they need to know the truth, and we need to realize that our proximity to them, if indeed we have tried to love them like Jesus does, is a blessing and an advantage, not a disadvantage. Even if you haven't been the greatest example of Jesus' love to them, be honest and make it right. Start now. Determine to love those in your community the same way Jesus loved those in His, and work to show them Christ so that your witness will be credible.

What do the words reasoning, disputing, persuading, and testifying mean, and where do they come into the picture?

I suppose this would be good to cover before we get too far since it's supposed to be the topic of this section...

- These are the words Luke uses to describe ***Paul's efforts*** throughout the book of Acts.
- Pay attention to what is taking place in each passage to get the best sense of each word.
  - o Acts 17:1–3: here we find several key words, but the one we are most interested in is ***"reason"***, which means to discuss with reasonable discourse, or "the use of words to ***exchange*** thoughts and ideas."[40]

Now when they had passed through Amphipolis and Apollonia, they came to Thessalonica, where was a *synagogue of the Jews: And Paul, as his manner was, went in unto them, and three sabbath days **reasoned** with them out of the scriptures, **Opening and alleging**, that Christ must needs have suffered, and risen again from the dead; and that this Jesus, whom I preach unto you, is Christ.[41]*

o   Acts 9:29: here we find Paul **"disputing"** with the Grecians. The word means "to seek or examine together," and signifies "to **discuss**."[42]

*"And he **spake boldly** in the name of the Lord Jesus, and disputed against the Grecians: but they went about to slay him."[43]*

NOTE: An interesting thought regarding Paul's interaction with the Grecians (considering that in the end they determined to slay him): do you think they were able to maintain their cool and simply discuss the issues? Probably not. Obviously, there was contention there, but that doesn't mean Paul was **contentious**. When a person is bested, their pride can flare up, at which point they typically become angry and unreasonable. This is sometimes unavoidable despite all efforts to the contrary.

o   Acts 19:8: In this passage Paul is disputing (same Greek word translated "reason" in Acts 17:2) and **persuading**, which means "bringing about a change of mind by the influence of reason or moral considerations."[44]

"And he went into the synagogue, and spake boldly for the space of three months, disputing and persuading the things concerning the kingdom of God."[45]

- o   I would also like to point out v.9 here.
  - ■ This shows Paul was not interested in arguing and fighting for the sake of mastery.
  - ■ He was interested in ***winning someone*** with the gospel; hence, the second they became hard and it was clear that there was no ground to be gained, he moved on.

"But when divers were hardened, and believed not, but spake evil of that way before the multitude, he departed from them, and separated the disciples, disputing daily in the school of one Tyrannus."[46]

NOTE: When I say Paul moved on, I don't mean in the sense of no longer caring (obviously his heart was broken for his people, the Jews), but in the sense of entrusting them to God and leaving the door open. Consider: in chapter 19 Paul is in Ephesus, but verse 1 points out that Apollos was in Corinth. Paul was in Corinth in chapter 18 and accomplished little with the Jews. When it became clear that they would no longer listen (v.6), he moved on. Yet, Apollos went back, and where Paul struggled, Apollos did well. The idea is to leave the door open for someone else. Don't do irreparable damage with your importunity.

- o   Acts 28:23–24: here we have Paul settled into his home in Rome.
  - ■ He was apparently on some sort of house arrest.
  - ■ While there, many of the chief Jews came to him.

It was to these people that he "***testified***" and
expounded the kingdom of God, "persuading
them concerning Jesus."

- The word "testified" means, "testify, assert,
  declare, insist, ***emphatically [forcefully] state***,
  warn, admonish."[47]

And when they had appointed him a day, there came many
*to him into his lodging; to whom he expounded and **testified***
the kingdom of God, persuading them concerning Jesus,
both out of the law of Moses, and out of the prophets, from
*morning till evening. And some **believed** the things which*
*were spoken, and some **believed not**.*[48]

- Again, Luke paints a clear picture of this discourse for us, including the outcome.
- The result of this testimony from Paul was,
  "some believed ... and some believed not."
- Simple.

o Other passages that help us see Paul's approach to
  witnessing:
  - Acts 9:22
  - Acts 13:43
  - Acts 18:4, 19
  - Acts 24:24–25
  - Acts 26:8

- The words, 'reasoning, disputing, persuading, and testifying' all serve to help us see one thing – Paul's desire
  was to convince people.

o   If he could not, he was glad to leave them with something to consider.

o   Paul wasn't put out by questions and discussion.

o   Luke makes it plain that Paul reasoned with people, which implies give and take.

o   This is healthy.

o   His desire was to convince.

o   We have to understand that a person's faith has to be genuine.

o   A man convinced against his will is of the same opinion still.

o   We want people to come to Christ because they get it; because they truly believe.

o   This happens by reasoning together with them.

o   If they won't listen, or the conversation isn't going anywhere, then it is perfectly fine to leave them with something to consider.

o   Paul did this.

o   However, before it gets to that point, we have to be willing to do the work of reasoning with people, and understand it may take time to convince them, but as long as they are willing to discuss it, it's worth the effort.

o   Remember, not everyone will be ready to sign on the first time they hear the gospel.

o   I personally came to Christ two years after the first time I heard the gospel and had heard it several times in between.

o   Be willing to reason with them.

o   Welcome their questions and be patient.

So, if identifying a person's current spiritual condition, where they are and what they believe, is part of what equates to *charting a course*, reasoning is the equivalent of actually *leading* them on the journey.

Having taken the time to build a somewhat accurate spiritual profile of the individual, in that you have been able to identify where they are, it's time to get started.

NOTE: No matter what, getting the ball rolling will take a *deliberate effort* on your part, nine times out of ten. There is the rare occasion where a person is ready to be saved and so they will be the one that begins directing the conversation toward spiritual things, but that is the exception, not the rule.

Also, keep in mind, gathering information is usually pretty easy. The opportunity for contention comes when we begin actually trying to lead them on the journey. In our efforts to reconcile them to the Father through Christ, we will likely have to meet their current beliefs head-on.

- Now that we are ready to get started, understand that there are basically two sources from which we are free to reason and testify, both of which are forms of revelation—God revealing Himself to man.
  o *Creation*: natural or general revelation.
    - Psalms 19:1-6

NOTE: Before you scoff at the idea of reasoning from God's natural revelation of Himself, consider the psalmist's words regarding the universal language the creation speaks: "There is no speech nor language, where their voice is not heard. Their line is gone out through all the earth, and their words to the end of the world" (Psalms 19:3–4a).

- Romans 1:19–20
- The details of creation can be quite effective when you consider and observe all that is there (which is impossible).
  - The heavens and the earth and the depths of the oceans and seas (of which we know less about than we do the surface of the moon or Mars) all point to a ***Creator***.
  - The biological complexities of all living things make a strong case for design and the necessity of a designer.
  - The ***universal*** and ***inherent*** moral nature of man also presents a strong case for a moral Source that exists apart from and outside of our natural world – a world within which we find no explanation for morality in the natural sense.
- The creation is the best place to start with those who are atheists, or with those who believe in a deity other than Jehovah God, as this is the perfect way to introduce Him.
- Good ***questions*** can go far in helping them see the weaknesses of their belief system, whatever it is.
- This will take time, as the questions need time to ***create doubt*** in their deeply rooted, firmly established, currently held beliefs, thus ***making room*** for faith.

o Following are some good resources for this type of study and preparation:

Disclaimer: I can't endorse everything you will read from the following authors and books or from the videos I am going to recommend. I can say much, if not most, of what you will find here will be great and helpful. I will simply say to read and watch with the determination to try everything by the Scriptures. If you do that, you will be fine, and your witness will be better for it.

- *Darwin's Black Box* and *The Edge of Evolution* both by Michael J. Behe
- *The Case for a Creator* by Lee Strobel
- Any of the videos from *The Institute for Creation Research,* otherwise known as *ICR.*
- *The Discovery Institute* also has a website where several good videos can be found; two of my favorites from that site being *Revolutionary,* which is about Michael J. Behe, and *The Information Enigma,* which features geneticist Dr. Douglas Axe.
- The point is, the resources are out there, and the effort to reach people is worth the work.

NOTE: Please understand that watching or reading any of the material presented here does not make you an expert in the various scientific fields you will learn about. So many Christians are so arrogant about things they really know very little about. The point isn't to be able to show people how little they actually know or how laughable their current beliefs are. The point is to be able to help people see that you take your faith very seriously and that indeed it is a well-reasoned and informed faith. I have learned that being able to ask the right questions can bolster the credibility of your faith and compromise the structural integrity of the bedrock of belief that already exists in the minds of many. <u>All it takes is a little doubt to create room for faith.</u>

So, there is creation itself that we are free to reason from, and there is . . .

- o ***Scripture***: special revelation (I don't think we need passages to support our use of Scripture in preaching the gospel).
  - Suffice it to say that Scripture is alive, and it is powerful.
  - We can trust in its ability, along with the work of the Spirit of God, to accomplish in the mind and the heart of man what we cannot.
  - Going straight to the Scriptures is best for those who believe in Jehovah God but are not saved.
  - They may be members of a cult or have other religious affiliations under the umbrella of Christianity.
- o Paul reasons from both creation and Scripture as we have seen in other sections.

NOTE: Paul also uses his personal experience, his ***testimony***, or what happened to him personally. While this can be effective, we have to be careful here. If we rely on this too much, we risk making our faith this entirely subjective thing. We can give the impression that it's all relative to a person's experience. At that point, "what happened to you is good for you, but that isn't what happened for me, and my testimony is just as good as yours," can be the result. It is important that we use our testimony in conjunction with Scripture when we are able. The reason I say when we are able is because I do not believe a person should pass up an opportunity to witness simply because they haven't mastered the Scriptures yet. If all you have currently is your testimony, then by all means use it, but continue to grow in the Word so that you can substantiate your testimony with the Truth of God's Word.

Conclusion:

All need to be saved, and salvation is the same for all, but not all are in the same place regarding their ability to appreciate that need. Like Paul, we need to be ready to confront them through ***reasoning***, ***disputing***, ***persuading***, and ***testifying*** in an effort to convince them of the truth of the gospel.

- We need to love people and care about them enough to get to know them.
- We need to try to get a feel for where they are spiritually, so that we can determine the ***best way*** to help them see their need for Christ.
- We need to then look and pray for an opportunity to engage them on the matter, reasoning from both creation and the Scriptures (ultimately, you will move from creation to the Scripture to the gospel – beginning with creation simply puts you a step back in the order).
- We need to be ***sensitive*** not to overdo it.
  - o When they are ready to be done, let them be done.

o   You must look at this as a ***marathon*** instead of a sprint.
o   It is great when a person trusts Christ the first time you witness to them, but you have to leave the door open for future opportunities, if it becomes clear that they are not yet ready.
o   Remember, we can and should take no for an answer.
o   Leave the high-pressure stuff to door-to-door salespeople.

And last but not least . . .

- We need to walk away from a fight and preferably before it gets that far.
    o   We are trying to ***reason***, which requires two parties.
    o   If they shut down, or are no longer receptive, or begin to get angry, you are no longer reasoning.
    o   We are confronting.
    o   We have to ***speak the truth***.
    o   We must contend, but we are not to be contentious.

In Paul's own words, "Follow peace with all men, and holiness, without which no man shall see the Lord (Hebrews 12:14)."

WITNESSING LIKE PAUL: SECTION 6

The Doctrine of Salvation

—⁂—

Section Aim

The purpose of section six is to equip people, from Scripture, with an in-depth knowledge and understanding of the doctrine of salvation.

NOTE: I would not recommend trying to present this information to a lost person in its entirety. This is more of a resource for you to draw from as needed. No doubt you will be confronted at times with questions, and hopefully this information will help, but just to reiterate, this is not a "soul-winning plan" that I am presenting in this section.

The Doctrine of Salvation

"For by grace are you saved through faith; and that not of yourselves: it is the gift of God: Not of works, lest any man should boast."
The Apostle Paul

"Search the Scriptures; for in them ye think ye have eternal life: and they are they which testify of me."
Jesus of Nazareth

The first thing we have to deal with is our _sin_.

Please understand that we are not going to go as in-depth as we could, but we are going into greater depth than you are likely going to want to take a lost or unchurched person.

- We are all **_born_** sinners.
  - o Adam and Eve sinned and experienced spiritual death immediately and subjected themselves, and the entire human race, to **_physical_** death (Genesis 2:16–17; 3:6-7).
  - o Because of their sin, the entire human race is born **_spiritually_** dead and bound to sin (Genesis 5:1–3, Psalm 51:5, Romans 5:12, 14, 15a, 17a, 18a, 19a, Ephesians 2:1–3), thus "by nature."

NOTE: I have heard it explained this way and I have used this as well. I have asked people in an attempt to help them embrace what they are: "What do you call a person that bats?" The answer is obviously a batter. "What do you call a person that runs?" To which the proper response is a runner. Then I would ask, "What do you call a person that sins?" They would say a sinner. While I understand the point and purpose of such an exercise, it isn't an entirely accurate representation of our situation. We are not sinners because we sin. The solution would then be to simply stop sinning. We **_sin_** because we are **_sinners_**, and hence, on our own we cannot stop sinning.

The proper way to illustrate this truth is to imagine that you were born as a slave with a slave master. This slave master is the part of your nature that is inclined to sin. It is your sin nature. This sinful nature drives you. Not everything you do is wicked or sinful, but everything is corrupted to some degree in a sinful manner by this propensity within you. You are bound, chained to, and shackled with sin.

When you trust Christ, the old slave master of your sin nature does not go away. It is simply that you are no longer obligated to him. You now have a new master. You can still choose to serve the old nature, the old slave master, but you are also free to serve another master; a new master.

So, we sin because it is what we are; we are born sinners. It's our nature to go our own way. It's our nature to live independent of God.

The effects of sin upon the race of man are explained well by Evans in his book, *The Great Doctrines of the Bible:*

> The entire **_nature of man_**, mentally, morally, spiritually, physically, is sadly **_affected_** by sin.
> The understanding is darkened (Eph. 4:18; 1 Cor. 2:14); the heart is deceitful and wicked (Jer. 17:9, 10); the mind and conscience are defiled (Gen. 6:5; Titus 1:15); the flesh and spirit are defiled (2 Cor. 7:5); the will is enfeebled

(Rom. 7:18); and we are utterly destitute of any Godlike qualities which meet the requirements of God's holiness (Rom. 7:18).

What does all this mean? A.H. Strong, in his Systematic Theology, explains the matter somewhat as follows: It does not mean the entire absence of conscience (John 8:9); nor of all moral qualities (Mark 10:21); nor that men are prone to every kind of sin (for some sins exclude others). It does mean, however, that man is totally destitute of love to God which is the all absorbing commandment of the law (John 5:42); that the natural man has an aversion to God... that man is in possession of a nature that is constantly on the downgrade, and from the dominion of which he is totally unable to free himself (Rom. 7:18, 23).[49]

- Because we are all born sinners, we ***all have sinned*** (past tense, which means it is done; if we never committed another sin, it wouldn't matter). Old Testament: Psalms. 14:1–3; New Testament: Romans 3:9–10, 23.

NOTE: A good way to illustrate Romans 3:23 is by having someone imagine they were about to have a throwing contest with Nolan Ryan (if anyone even remembers who he is) at the Grand Canyon. The fact is that even though Nolan Ryan is going to throw much farther than they are, both of them are going to fall short.

When we compare ourselves to others, we may not look too bad. Others are not the standard though. God is. He is righteous and holy. Compared to Him, ***we all fall short***.

It is important for us to have a proper understanding of sin.

- Sin is **_anything_** that **_goes against_** God's law (1 John 3:4).
- There is no **_big_** or little sin (James 2:10).

NOTE: I like to illustrate this using a fence. I ask people if they are familiar with barbed wire fencing. I use it because it is one of the simplest fences to build, but any fence will do. We establish that each barbed wire fence consists basically of several fence posts spaced out evenly and barbed wire. Once these components are combined, you have a fence. Now I want to make it clear that regardless of how many fence posts you have, there is one fence. I then ask them if, in the presence of a "No Trespassing" sign, it matters which fence post they cross. Of course, it does not matter which post you cross because you have crossed the one fence. Each component is merely a part of the whole fence.

It is the same way with God's law. All these many commandments come together to form God's law. It doesn't matter which fence post—commandment—we break. By breaking any, we have broken God's law. We have thus sinned according to 1 John 3:4 and have thus earned sin's wage.

- Good does not **_erase_** prior sin because of current good, nor is good intended to outweigh sin.
  o Our righteousness is as filthy rags (Isa. 64:6).

NOTE: Imagine trying to offer a filthy rag (and if you study it out, the imagery is far more offensive than perhaps you realize) as payment to God for your sin so that He would then welcome you into fellowship with Him.

- o The purpose of the law (that which people try to abide by to merit heaven) is to establish our ***guilt*** (Romans 3:19–20, Gal. 2:16; 3:11; 24), not attain righteousness.
- o The bad is already there and does not go away, nor does God overlook it simply because there is ample good to counter it.
- o Such teaching is found nowhere in Scripture.

NOTE: The problem isn't a lack of good, but the ***presence of bad***. Something has to be done about the sin.

Sin has a wage.

It is not enough that we understand we are all sinners. We must also understand the ***effects*** of sin.

- • A wage is ***payment*** for work that has been done.
  - o We work for a wage.
  - o If we work and receive no money, we get upset because we earned that money; we deserve it because of what we have done.

- • Sin's wage is ***death*** (Romans 6:23).
  - o All mankind is born spiritually dead separated from God.
  - o All mankind experiences physical death.

(For more details and Scripture regarding both points, see heading "The first thing we have to deal with is our sin.")

NOTE: As we have shown already, these are both due to Adam's sin in the garden, but that is not where the wage ends as is indicated in Hebrews 9:27.

   o   All mankind is destined to receive *__eternal__* death.

If man dies separated from God by sin on this earth, he will remain separated from God for all eternity in a place called the *__Lake__* of Fire (Romans 6:23, Revelation 21:8).

So, to recap:

We are born spiritually dead, separated from God. We are born bound by sin and to sin because of our sinful nature. This happened as a result of the fall in the garden. We are all sinners and therefore have all sinned. If we remain in our sinful, spiritually dead state, however, we will experience eternal death in the Lake of Fire separated from God for all eternity when this physical life ends.

It is important that people understand this is the plight of all mankind, which includes them personally.

"But the gift of God . . ."

The Gift of God

It wouldn't be much of a gospel (good news) if it ended back at the wages of sin. . .

NOTE: The wages of sin is death *__spiritually__*, *__physically__*, and *__eternally__*. We cannot avoid being born spiritually dead, nor can we escape physical death, but we do not have to remain spiritually dead and separated from God, nor do we need to experience eternal death because God offers us a ***gift***!

- God has offered a gift (Romans 6:23).
  - o A gift and a wage are two different things.
  - o You have to work in order to be worthy of a wage.
  - o A gift, however, is ***payed for by someone else***, making it free to you.

NOTE: Think of Christmas. All of those presents are paid for by someone, but they are free to you.

- "The gift of God is ***eternal life*** . . ."
  - o We are born spiritually dead and separated from God.
  - o Jesus makes us ***spiritually alive*** complete with a ***new birth*** and ***reconciles*** us to God (John 3:1-17, 2 Corinthians 5:17–21, Ephesians 2:1).

NOTE: Evans has a great word on this point:

> Regeneration is the impartation of a new and divine life; a new creation; the production of a new thing. It is Genesis 1:26 over again. It is not the old nature altered, reformed, or re-invigorated, but a new birth from above. This is the teaching of such passages as John 3:3-7; 5:21, Ephesians 2:1; 10, 2 Corinthians 5:17.
>
> By nature, man is dead in sin (Eph. 2:1); the new birth imparts new life – the life of God, so that henceforth he is as those that are alive from the dead; he has passed out of death into life (John 5:24).[50]

- o We receive this life the ***instant*** we trust in Christ, so it is something that saved people have and benefit from now, not something they will have some day (1 John 5:11–13).
- o This life is eternal (John 3:16, 1 John 5:13, Ephesians 1:13-14, 1 Peter 1:5).
  - It can ***never*** end in any way for any reason.
  - When this physical life ends, we will continue to live in heaven with God for eternity (2 Cor. 5:8).

- This gift of eternal life was given "***through*** Jesus Christ our Lord."
  - o God's love, mercy, and grace rise up to meet His holiness, righteousness, and justness.
  - o In Jesus all are fulfilled (John 3:16; Romans 5:8)!

NOTE: Understand that ***Jesus is God***! He is God the Son. He is just as much God as God the Father. They are one according to Jesus (John 1:1–14; 10:30; 14:9, 1 John 5:7).

- o Jesus was the ***propitiation*** (Romans 3:24-25, 1 John 2:2; 4:10).
  - God could not simply excuse sin.
  - He is righteous and just.
  - To overlook sin would compromise both of those attributes.
  - Therefore, payment must be made.
  - Jesus was the satisfactory payment.
  - Jesus' shed blood and separation from the Father on the cross satisfies the wrath and the righteousness of God on our behalf.

o He brought *__justification__* (Romans 3:24; 28; 5:1; 9, 1 Corinthians 6:11, Galatians 2:16, Titus 3:7).

Through justification, we are declared righteous, not as though we have sinned and are now clean, but as if there was never any sin to begin with (Hebrews 8:12, Psalms 103:12, Isaiah 43:25).

o He *__became__* sin (2 Corinthians 5:21, Isaiah 53:2–6).
o He *__takes__* sin away (John 1:29, Hebrews 9–10; 10:4).

• Receiving the Gift
  o God has presented us with a gift.
  o It has been made available to us, but we have to choose to receive it.

How does a person do that?

o The gift of eternal life was given through Jesus and is found in Jesus (1 John 5:11–13).

This life is in the Son, and so if you want this life, you have to receive the Son! Paul explains more clearly than anyone, in my opinion, what it takes to receive the Son.

NOTE: Eternal life is a benefit of *__trusting__* Christ. Trusting Christ needs to be the point. He is God in the flesh! He is the One and only true God. He is the *__Way__*, the *__Truth__*, and the *__Life__*. No man can come to *__God__*, but by Him (John 14:1–6, Acts 4:12; 8:36–37, Romans 3, Ephesians 2:8–9).

o   We must hear or be **_confronted_** with the gospel in some way, believe in Jesus—who He is and the sufficiency of what He has done—and thus call on Him to be our Savior (Romans 10:13–14).

o   Whosoever does this **_shall_** be saved (Romans 10:13, John 3:16).

NOTE: Again, because of Rom. 10:14, I am inclined to encourage a person to ask Jesus to save them, but am not convinced that an outward, verbal request is entirely necessary due to other passages in Scripture. Also, if a person is just saying, "Yes I believe in Jesus and believe that He is the only Savior" and thus they ask Him to save them simply because they don't want to go to the Lake of Fire, then I would exercise caution. We receive salvation by trusting in Jesus as the Savior. **_Anything less_** than genuine faith in Him, and in His work on our behalf simply will not do.

o   It was provided though Jesus and can only be received through Jesus.

o   A person must **_hear_**, **_believe_**, and **_call_** (receive).

Conclusion:

- We are all born sinners.
- Because we are all born sinners, we all have sinned.
  o   Sin is anything that goes against God's law.
  o   There is no big or little sin.
  o   Good does not erase prior sin, nor is good intended to outweigh sin.

- A wage is payment for work that has been done.
- Sin's wage is death.
- God has offered a gift.
- "The gift of God is eternal life . . ."
- This gift of eternal life was given "through Jesus Christ our Lord."
- We receive this gift by trusting in Jesus, who He is and what He has done for us on the cross.

WITNESSING LIKE PAUL: SECTION 7

Concluding Remarks

—◦◦◦—

Section Aim

The purpose of this section is to wrap up the series by summarizing the content and offering some practical tips moving forward. We have a wonderful example in the apostle Paul, but now it's time to apply what we've learned.

Concluding Remarks

"Churches that have lost their heart for evangelism are living out their final chapter."
Anthony G. Pappas

Series Review

- Paul was a man who trusted Christ, ***gave his life*** to the effort of sharing the gospel with everyone, everywhere, and was mightily used of God to that end.

He, like any other servant of God, was human, nothing more and nothing less. That ought to encourage every one of us. If God could use Paul to the degree that He did, who is to say or what is to say that He can't use you and me in a similar fashion?

- Paul had a heart for the lost that ***knew no bounds***.

In my opinion, this is one of the most distinguishing characteristics regarding the apostle Paul. His heartbeat for the lost of this world. He was broken for them.

- Not only did Paul have a heart broken for the lost, but he was convinced the gospel was ***sufficient***, not just to save the lost, but to convince the lost to trust in Christ.
- In addition, Paul saw himself as personally indebted to the lost of this world regarding the gospel, which in turn gave Paul great boldness in presenting the gospel to others.

- The fact that all need to be saved, and salvation is the same for all, but not all are in the same place regarding their ability to appreciate that need, caused Paul to *__adjust__* his approach to the gospel accordingly in his efforts to convince them of the truth through reasoning, disputing, persuading, and testifying.
- Paul had a mastery of the gospel, and the truth is, God is clear in His Word regarding the matter of salvation, thus we as believers *__ought to be clear__* on the matter that we might be able to clearly convey it to others.

Practical Tips

- Begin with *__love__*.

We need to be fully acquainted with God's love for us so that we can be ready to love *__others__* properly. Our desire should stem from a genuine concern for others. Paul was broken for people. He loved them. Do you genuinely love them? Begin there. Think of them.

Consider Matthew 22:26–40. Jesus says the greatest commandment in the law—in other words, if we are to concern ourselves with just one thing this would be it—love God with all that we are, with every ounce of our being.

In an effort to help drive this point home, consider that, in my opinion, Scripture bears out that man is a tripartite being. One part of man's nature is his soul. In reality, man is a soul. The soul is the person of man. It is that which makes you, you. It is the eternal aspect of man. If the body dies or the spirit is never made alive or quickened, the soul of man still lives on separated from God for eternity. The soul of man is where we find the capacity for thinking and reasoning, it is where we find the will of man, and it is where we find man's emotions. Words that are used interchangeably in Scripture for the soul or various aspects of the soul are heart and mind, among others. Jesus' use of these three words is interesting as each one can be associated to one of the three aspects of the soul. Mind can be said to refer to the thinking and reasoning of man. Heart can be linked to the emotions of man. Soul can be linked to the will of man—the vital aspect with all of its desires. Jesus' use of these three words can be viewed as an emphasis on His part regarding the entirety with which man is to be devoted to God. In another book, this same account is recorded, and Jesus even includes the body: that thing through which man relates to the natural world. So, the point is that Jesus says the first and great commandment is that we be devoted to God with all that we are.

So, Jesus says the first and great commandment has to do with our devotion to God the Father. The second, though, is horizontal in nature rather than vertical. It has to do with our ***devotion to man***. Jesus makes it clear that the designation of neighbor isn't based on one's proximity to our dwelling. According to the example given in the parable of the Good Samaritan, we determine who our neighbors are not by any action on their part, but by our actions toward them.

So, when Jesus says to love your neighbor as yourself, He is saying to love man in general—all man, in the same manner that we love ourselves. We know we love ourselves by the care we take in meeting our own needs and desires. Careful consideration of this point will help you see the incredibly tall order that has been placed upon us. Jesus says, to the same degree that you care for you, care for others. To the same degree that you love you, love others. It's a big deal. In our church, the way we try to think about this, is in regard to Jesus' example. Our goal is to try to show love to our community the same way Jesus showed love to His. He is the perfect example of this concept. Paul is a great example as well. Think about all Paul sacrificed in his effort to get the gospel to others.

By the way, Paul's effort to get the gospel to others wasn't merely a matter of fulfilling some objective he received, and so he went about coldly dispensing his duty until all had heard and he could move on to something else. No, Paul loved people and operated out of that love. Just like Jesus, Paul served people in general because he loved people in general. Please don't miss this. The gospel naturally flowed out of that as something you'd want anyone you love to know about. But to say you love people and not be moved by their struggles or challenges, and not feel compelled to help, is a gigantic inconsistency that calls into question the veracity of your "love!" Begin with love. Serve those around you. Be a help and a blessing and take the gospel with you! Jesus did this. Just read the gospels and see for yourself. Paul did as well. He healed people (Acts 14, 16, 20, and 28). He prayed for the safety of others (27:21-26). He worked to care for those that were shipwrecked with him after they washed up on the island of Malta (Acts 28:1-3). Now, about the situation in Malta, regarding the bundle of sticks that Paul placed on the fire, try to consider that this wasn't some small campfire. This was a fire intended to warm and dry almost 300 drenched grown men. The idea behind the word "bundle" means more than just a handful. Paul was working to keep a large fire stoked which would have required, not just one trip with a few sticks, but many trips with logs. Paul was in his fifties, at least by this point. He was also weary. He was also cold. He was also tired, and he was likely one of the oldest guys in the group, yet he is serving. Begin with love.

NOTE: As a part of this, ***get to know them***. Focus on them in your conversation. Ask them questions about themselves. Every time you want to say something about you, stop, think, and try to ask something about them instead. Don't be weird about this. If they are asking about you then answer, but remember, we are trying to focus on them in an effort to love them.

Begin with ***love***. Don't beat yourself up if you have trouble in this area. We all do. We all need the Lord's help in this way. Let us ask Him, and then proceed accordingly, trusting that He will enable us along the way. You will mess up. You will have awkward and uncomfortable moments, but that will help you, not hurt you in the long run. You really do get points for trying. When people see that you are trying to love them, it goes a long way.

- Be ***patient***.

Most people will not trust Christ or even be willing to discuss such things openly ***at first***. Nor will they be willing to consider differences in a civil manner without getting defensive ***at first***. It will take a while for them to get to the place where they trust you enough to come to you with a real desire to hear and understand. There were times when Paul spent months and even years in one place trying to reason with people about the gospel. Be patient and be gentle. Start by trying to find ways to talk about the Lord's work in your life. Talk occasionally about prayers answered. Look for opportunities to lift up the Lord and His love and goodness. Look for opportunities to pray for this person. Look for opportunities where they might even be willing to allow you to pray with them. Try to connect them with people from the church in non-committal settings. Avoid settings that might make them uncomfortable. In other words, inviting them to church is great, but spend time with them outside of church. Have them **_over to your place_** and have one or two people from the church over as well, and just do something fun. Serve them. The idea, again, is that you are in this for the long haul. It is about them and the need of their soul. You see it this way because you love them. So be patient. Do not ever be pushy, forceful, condemning, or rude. For real; rudeness is never justified, necessary, effective, or even right.

NOTE: Now, obviously this pertains to those within your current and regular sphere of influence. When it comes to witnessing to someone on the subway, or on a plane, you won't have nearly as much time. The principle of being patient and practically loving them first still applies. You just don't have as much time.

• Be **_sensitive_**.

Be sensitive to people and to the Holy Spirit. Look for clues in a person's words or body language that say you might need to back off. Understand that they perhaps do not have the same preconceptions that you have by virtue of a different social environment. That which has influenced their thinking may be different. If your goal is simply to prove them wrong and yourself right, that is one thing. If your goal is to show them the love of Christ and expose them to the gospel under the most beneficial circumstances possible with regard to potential fruitfulness because you love them and want to see them get saved, then be patient and sensitive to where they are religiously, philosophically, and spiritually. Remember that they are incapable of seeing things the way you do or understanding them the way that you do by virtue of your possession of the Holy Spirit of God and perspective. Be sensitive to the fact that people without Christ live and think and act the same way you would without Christ and the way you probably still do, to a degree and at different times, even with Christ.

Also listen to the Spirit as He leads. As you sense Him directing, trust Him and follow His leadership. Let Him open the doors and walk through them when He does.

Be sensitive to the appropriateness of the occasion. The bathroom is probably an inappropriate time even though the argument could be made that for at least a few moments you have a captive audience. During work hours may not be good timing. Things like that need to be considered. With that in mind . . .

- Be ___available___.

How serious is your desire to reason with someone about the gospel? You went to them and they weren't ready. Do you care enough to make yourself available for the opportunities they do give you?

When they need you, be there. They went to a party and got in over their head. They need to know that they can count on you. If that means picking them up and taking them home, then fine. They got into trouble with the law. Use your head and don't break the law, but be ready to help them as you can. They need someone to talk to at three in the morning. Be there. They lost a loved one, etc. Many people come to Christ through crisis.

Guys, it would be a good idea for you to set up real boundaries in this area regarding the opposite sex. The same goes for women. There need to be things that you are not willing to do; they need to be non-negotiable but have a plan. Have a friend that you can count on of the opposite sex that can step in when you need.

I'm sure there is more we could discuss here, but let's move on to one final tip.

K.I.S.S.

Remember that a person doesn't need to have a thorough understanding of the doctrine of salvation in order to be saved. So, let's keep it super simple. What did you think K.I.S.S. stands for?

- All have ***sinned***.
  - o   Romans 3:23; 5:12; 3:10, 1 John 3:4, James 2:10

- Sin has a ***wage***, which is separation from God in this life and the next.
  - o   Romans 6:23a, Hebrews 9:27, Revelation 21:8

- God loves you and wants to have a relationship with you, and so He is offering you a gift instead – the ***gift of eternal life***.
  - o   Romans 6:23b, John 3:16; 1 John 5:13

- This gift is given through the death, burial, and resurrection of His Son **_Jesus_**.
  - o   1 Corinthians 15:1–3, Romans 5:8, 1 John 4:10

So, this gift is given through Jesus, and...

- It is given to all who believe in Jesus and trust in His work on the cross!
  - o   1 John 5:11–13, Romans 10:13–14

If they are willing to hear, and upon hearing, they **_believe_** and trust in Him and His work on the cross, then Jesus will save them and reconcile them to God. You can pray with them at this point if you like, but the key is helping them understand that their relationship with God is dependent upon faith in Jesus – who He is and what He has done – and faith in Jesus alone.

- We have a good **_example_** before us in the apostle Paul.
  - o   Paul loved the Lord.
  - o   Paul loved people.
  - o   Paul lived to see man reconciled to God.

- We have the **_tools_** to do the job.
  - o   We have God's revelation of Himself through creation and through His Word.
  - o   We have the gospel.
  - o   We have the Holy Spirit of God.

- It's just a matter of going out and doing that which Jesus has called us to do.

"Being an extrovert isn't essential to evangelism; obedience and love are." Rebecca M. Pippert

Conclusion:

God loves people. He loves the people that you see every day. God wants to know them, and He wants them to know Him! He paid a great price to make that possible. Your friends, family, coworkers, and neighbors, they all need to know about that. The person behind the counter at the gas station, your child's coach, or teacher; they need to know.

They need to know God is seeking them. They need to know God loves them. They need to know who Jesus is. They need to know what He did for them and what's available to them as a result. What they need is a witness.

They need someone like Paul to come along who will have a heart that aches for them. They need someone that will love them. They need someone who will patiently and boldly reason with them and testify to them and strive to persuade them. They need someone who will work to reach them right where they are. They need someone who will take the time to learn and grow and develop an informed faith that is rooted and grounded in truth! They need a witness... like Paul. They have you. What will you do?

Appendix

—ɷ—

Have you ever finished something only to determine later there was something missing? Well, that is the cause for this appendix. It would have been quite a bit of work to, now, here at the end, go back and make sure this last segment flowed with the rest of the content without being repetitive since this last segment was just recently produced as the final message in our Acts series here at Forest Hills. Shortly after preaching this message, however, it occurred to me that it needed to be included as a final encouragement to everyone who makes it through this study to jump out there and find a way to do the very thing Jesus saved us to do – bring others to Him! So, I hope this is a help. I hope it is a challenge, and I hope it inspires you to find a way in a world that isn't conducive to life devoted to this work.

A Fitting End... Acts 28:16-31

You know, being about the gospel these days is hard. Both culture and society make it so.

For a society that has within its governing document provision for free speech, there are a lot of rules in neighborhoods, or in work environments, or places of education, etc. that restrict what you can say, or how you can say it. Definitions are fluid regarding hate speech. Our society is incredibly sensitive when it comes to things they disagree with or don't like to hear. They can be easily angered or offended; really, in a lot of ways, people today seem angry in general. It almost feels like some people are looking for a reason to be offended.

The media would have you believe that the term "Christianity" carries with it some negative connotation within our culture, and perhaps, in some areas, that may actually be the case. Christians are often portrayed as backwoods, uneducated, simple, weak, superstitious, shallow, petty, judgmental, ridiculous, fanatical...

My wife doesn't even tell people what I do for a living unless they ask, and I imagine she cringes inside when they ask. That's not because she is embarrassed or ashamed. It's because she wants to build a relationship with people through which she can work to reach them, and she calls it the conversation killer. As soon as it comes up, no matter how chatty the person was before, once she tells them what I do, she says it's like dousing the entire conversation with cold water. People often just shut down.

That very scenario has played out here over and over for her.

So how are you supposed to be about the gospel in a society that seems so conditioned, whether by firsthand experience or by hearsay, to distrust or disdain anything to do with religion or Jesus or Christianity: how do you live trying to get people to Jesus when circumstances seem so contrary to that effort?

Well, whether you believe it or not, our experience today wasn't foreign to Paul and the Christians of the first century. Paul's circumstances weren't always conducive to what he pursued in life.

So, what did he do?

Well, take a moment and read Acts 28:16-31.

I love the way Luke begins this section of chapter 28. "And when we came to Rome..." You get this sense of finality, like this is the final stretch of a long, unfolding drama, and it's about to come to an end.

Rome, obviously, held a special significance in the heart and mind of Paul, and Luke knew it, I think. In fact, I think any of the people who travelled and ministered with Paul would have known it. According to his letter to the Romans, Rome was a place that was on his mind quite regularly throughout his ministry for many years (Romans 1 and Romans 15). There were many times during his travels that Paul determined to go to Rome, but the Spirit led him elsewhere.

Now, after a long and dangerous voyage, they're here. I think you'll see that, like many times throughout the life and ministry of Paul, circumstances weren't ideal for the work that drew him to Rome in the first place.

- He was under house arrest.
- He was chained to a Roman soldier.
- He couldn't leave.
- And he was concerned that the Jews of that city had already been poisoned against him and 'this sect' he wanted to tell them about and the Jesus that he now followed.

So, what does Paul do?

Paul's circumstances have changed, but his desire to get people to Jesus and help them understand who He is, hasn't, and God's desire to see the gospel reach people hadn't!

So, what does Paul do?

Well, Paul never let his circumstances change what he was about. Instead, he simply changed how he went about it.

- All throughout Paul's life as a follower of Jesus and his ministry Paul was about one thing – getting the gospel to people and helping them understand who Jesus is and why it mattered (v.16-31, key – v.17).
  - o That is exactly what we see him setting up here in the text.
  - o Paul is in Rome for three days (v.16-17), when he invites the chief of the Jews (more prominent Jews, or leaders – more influential within the Jewish community) together to his home.
  - o It's interesting, but not only is he still doing what he's always done – he still follows this same pattern of Jew first and then Gentile.
  - o This is the first of two meetings, the purpose of which is to feel things out and figure out where everyone is (remember that Paul was contextually sensitive in his approach) before setting up the second meeting at which he begins to try and help them understand who Jesus is and why He came.

- However, as I've already stated, his circumstances are a little different, and so the way he goes about reaching out to them is a little different.
  - o All throughout the Book of Acts we see Paul going to people in general and to the Jews specifically.
  - o Not only did he travel from town to town, but every time he came to a new town he went where? To the synagogue.
    - When he came to Philippi, there was no synagogue.
    - So, he finds out where the few Jews living in Philippi gathered, and he goes there.
  - o He always went to people.
  - o Here in Rome, he couldn't do that.
  - o He couldn't go to them.
  - o He was chained to a guard and imprisoned in his own home.

Just consider this for a minute. In Romans 15 Paul makes it clear that this desire to go to Rome and minister to the saints there and preach the gospel has been on his heart for many years, and that many times throughout his ministry he determined to head that way. He is finally here. He finally made it, though the way he got there wasn't at all what he expected, and there were times he doubted if it would even happen at all (Acts 23:11). He's here, but it doesn't matter because he's caged inside his own house. All of Rome is right outside his door, but he can't get to them.

What does he do?

Paul didn't allow his circumstances to change what he was about. He simply changed the way he went about it. He couldn't go to them, but God had made it so that Paul had a good bit of liberty within the confines of his home, in that the Romans allowed him to have people over. So, if he couldn't go to Rome, he'd try his best to get Rome to come to him, and that's what he did! I truly think this is the best example of the heart of Paul regarding the gospel. His determination is evident here, possibly more than anywhere. For two years he continued this way in Rome. This is the way he did it.

I remember when we came to Rockville to start Forest Hills. We began meeting in a school. I wondered at times what people in our community would think about that. Would anyone come?

I have to imagine that those thoughts went through the mind of Paul. Think about it. He is obviously concerned that the Jews from Judaea had already sent letters or representatives to warn the Jews in Rome about Paul. So, he doesn't even know what the Jews of this region think of him, and the best he can do is send someone out to invite them to his home. I bet he wondered who would even show up. Do you see what I mean? And then to have his entire work there operate this way. How discouraging that could have been, but the work needed to be done. It had to happen. People needed to hear. He couldn't do it the way he preferred, but he had to do it nonetheless, and so he found a way. He did the best he could with what he had, and God blessed!

We are so easily deterred. How many of us let the slightest possibility of opposition or a technicality, or rule stop us alto-gether? "Well, I can't witness at work." "I can't talk about God or the Bible at school." "My neighbors would probably be irritated with me if I brought something like that up." "It would make things awkward or weird." "I don't want them to think I'm a religious fanatic or anything. That's what other people think of church people after all." "I don't want to start a fight." "They might get offended or upset." "It's just not socially acceptable." So, we resort to closet Christianity. We don't say anything. We don't even try.

Our 21st century, post-modern, increasingly secular culture isn't the most ideal backdrop for a life devoted to the work of the gospel, but it's our backdrop, nonetheless.

David Thomas said of the end of this account, "This is the last account we have of the great apostle. His biographer takes leave of him here. Here the curtain falls and hides the greatest actor. The greatest lives have a close."[51]

- Paul's done.
  - o He's gone.
  - o He served his generation.
  - o This is ours.
  - o Who's going to tell them how much God loves them and what He's done for them?

It's not easy to live for the gospel in our day and time, but like Paul, we must not let our circumstances change what we're about. We simply have to be determined and wise enough to go about it in a way that works with our generation.

We can't change what we're about, what God saved us to live for, but our circumstance may demand that we change the way we go about it.

- We have to be devoted to the gospel enough to find a way.
- We have to take seriously the work of both accurately representing Jesus in our world and repairing the

reputation of Christianity that has been marred by the misrepresentations and the misconceptions of others.

o   Please stop trying to fit into someone else's mold, and stop being unnecessarily weird or unapproachable...

NOTE: The goal of a believer isn't to try and stand out in our culture as much as possible. The goal is to be conformed to the image of Jesus. Standing out, becoming light, becoming salt, those come with the territory of being transformed by the renewing of your mind. It's a shame that what has turned some people away from the gospel isn't the plausibility of the gospel, but a representation of what Christianity looks like that isn't anything like Jesus.

o   Take your Bible, turn to the gospels, and just read.

o   Meet Jesus over again.

o   Take your eyes off of whatever Christian culture you've been brought up in and just look to Him.

o   See Him as He is, and let His example shape you.

o   Read the Book of Acts, and watch authentic Christianity unfold.

o   We try so hard to represent so many things.

o   We try to represent a denomination or group or movement.

- We try so hard to represent a certain school.
- We try so hard to identify with a particular group or brand of Christianity or Christian culture.
- We try to live up to the expectations or standards of others.
- Or, we try so hard not to identify with certain things.

o   This world needs to see Jesus... Period.

• We have to work to develop the type of informed faith that will enable us to engage our society in meaningful gospel-oriented dialogue.

And, ...

• We have to be willing to put ourselves out there at the risk of being mocked or ridiculed or singled out or shunned, or whatever...

Conclusion:

Just a word of encouragement as we close here... You know what Paul found regarding his concerns? That, at least in this situation, they were unfounded. Their response to him was that they hadn't heard anything about him. And regarding this sect? They were actually quite curious since it was spoken against everywhere. For them, this was an opportunity to learn more from the horse's mouth, so to speak. Paul gladly obliged. Some believed, and some didn't, but they had that opportunity because Paul refused to let his circumstance change what he was about. He found a way.

I think the more we follow Jesus and let Him shape us; the more we actually work to represent Him, and be to others what He is to us to the best of our ability, the more reasonable we'll be, the more well-reasoned we'll be, and the less threatening we'll be to a world that, I think, is still full of curious people when it comes to Christ and Christianity – people that can be reasoned with.

Perhaps this world and Christians have this in common. Maybe our perceptions and assumptions regarding each other aren't always fair or accurate. When we assume that they'll reject the gospel without giving them a chance we are guilty of judging them.

There are people out there that are open and curious. They just need someone willing to find a way to broach the topic in a world that isn't always conducive to the effort.

Again, they need someone like Paul. They have you. You have to find a way. What are you going to do?

Endnotes

1   Wiersbe, Warren W. "Acts." *The Wiersbe Bible Commentary: The Complete New Testament in One Volume*, David C. Cook, 2007, p. 350.

2   Roth, Carolyn. "Claudius, A Roman Commander." *Bible Characters*, 23 June 2016, obscurecharacters.com/2013/12/17/232/.

3   Orr, James, M.A., D.D., et al. "Claudius Lysias Definition and Meaning - Bible Dictionary." *Bible Study Tools*, 1915, www.biblestudytools.com/dictionary/claudius-lysias/.

4   Timeline. "The History of the Spanish Language." Tiki-Toki Timeline Maker: Beautiful Web-based Timeline Software, 06, www.tiki-toki.com/timeline/entry/135292/The-History-of-the-Spanish-language/#vars!panel=1298604!. Accessed 18 June 2019.

5   Wiersbe, Warren W. "Philippians." *The Wiersbe Bible Commentary: The Complete New Testament in One Volume*, David C. Cook, 2007, p. 645.

6   Thomas, David. "Section Twenty-Eighth - Acts ix. 1-19 - The Conversion of Saul." *Acts of the Apostles: A Homiletic Commentary*, Baker Book House, 1956, pp. 131-132.

7   Morse, Greg. "Over Our Dead Bodies: Embracing the Costs of Warning the Lost." *Desiring God*, 24 May 2018, www.desiringgod.org/articles/over-our-dead-bodies.

8   Wiersbe, Warren W. "Romans." *The Wiersbe Bible Commentary: The Complete New Testament in One Volume*, David C. Cook, 2007, p. 433.

9   "G331 - anathema – Strong's Greek Lexicon (KJV)" Blue Letter Bible. Web. 21 May, 2018. <https://www.blueletterbible.org//lang/Lexicon/Lexicon.cfm?Strongs=G331&t=KJV>.

10   "Calculating the Time and Cost of Paul's Missionary Journeys « OpenBible. info Blog." *OpenBible.info*, www.openbible.info/blog/2012/07/calculating-the-time-and-cost-of-pauls-missionary-journeys/.

11   Spurgeon, CH, et al. "First Sermons at New Park Street Chapel." *CH Spurgeon's Autobiography CH Spurgeon's Autobiography: Compiled from His Diary, Letters, and Records*, Passmore and Alabaster, 1889, p. 329.

12   Rainer, Thom S. "Introduction: Why Justin Is Not Like Jane Is Not Like Jack." *The Unchurched Next Door: Understanding Faith Stages As Keys to Sharing Your Faith*, Zondervan, 2003, p. 24.

13   …(Rainer, *Why Justin Is Not Like Jane Is Not Like Jack* 25).

14   …(Rainer, *Why Justin Is Not Like Jane Is Not Like Jack* 25).

15   …(Rainer, *Why Justin Is Not Like Jane Is Not Like Jack* 25).

16   Phillips, John. "Prologue." *Exploring Romans: An Expository Commentary*, Kregel Publications, 2002, p. 18.

17   Romans 1:15b–16

18   "Def Bold Search." *Google*, www.google.com/search?q=def+bold&rlz=1C1CHBF_enU-S794US794&oq=def+bold&aqs=chrome..69i57j0j69i-65j69i60l2j0.1639j0j7&sourceid=chrome&{google:instantExtend-edEnabledParameter}ie=UTF-8.

19   Phillips, John. "Prologue." *Exploring Romans: An Expository Commentary*, Kregel Publications, 2002, p. 19.

20   "Who is Felix in the Bible?" *GotQuestions.org*, www.gotquestions.org/Felix-in-the-Bible.html.

21   Pfeiffer, Charles F., et al. "Festus, Porcius." *Wycliffe Bible Dictionary*, Hendrickson Pub, 1998, pp. 605-606.

22 "Agrippa II." New World Encyclopedia, . 9 Feb 2019, 16:33 UTC. 30 May 2019, 15:39 <//www.newworldencyclopedia.org/p/index. php?title=Agrippa_II&oldid=1018027>.

23 The Editors of Encyclopaedia Britannica. "Herod Agrippa II." *Encyclopedia Britannica*, Encyclopædia Britannica, inc., 1 Jan. 2019, www.britannica.com/biography/Herod-Agrippa-II.

24 "Who Was Herod Agrippa II?" *GotQuestions.org*, www.gotquestions. org/Herod-Agrippa-II.html.

25 Brann, M. "AGRIPPA II." *JewishEncyclopedia.com*, The Kopelman Foundation, www.jewishencyclopedia.com/articles/913-agrippa-ii.

26 "G3781 - opheiletēs - Strong's Greek Lexicon (KJV)." Blue Letter Bible. Web. 10 Jun, 2018. <https://www.blueletterbible.org//lang/ Lexicon/Lexicon.cfm?Strongs=G3781&t=KJV>.

27 "Ashamed." *Merriam-Webster.com*. Merriam-Webster, n.d. Web. 5 July 2018.

28 *The Princess Bride*. Directed by Rob Reiner, Perf. Cary Elwes, Mandy Patinkin, Robin Wright. 1987. Act III Communications, 1987.

29 Vine, W. "Communicate, Communication - Vine's Expository Dictionary of New Testament Words." Blue Letter Bible. 24 Jun, 1996. Web. 17 May, 2019. <https://www.blueletterbible.org/search/ Dictionary/viewTopic.cfm>.

30 Keller, Timothy. "Preaching Christ From All Scripture." Preaching: Communicating Faith in an Age of Skepticism, Penguin, 2015, pp. 71-72.

31 "G2644 - katallassō - Strong's Greek Lexicon (KJV)." Blue Letter Bible. Web. 8 Jul, 2018. <https://www.blueletterbible.org//lang/ Lexicon/Lexicon.cfm?Strongs=G2644&t=KJV>.

32 Ibid.

33 "Expiation." Merriam-Webster.com. Merriam-Webster, n.d. Web. 8 July 2018.

34 Vine, W. "Propitiation - Vine's Expository Dictionary of New Testament Words." Blue Letter Bible. 24 Jun, 1996. Web. 8 Jul, 2018. <https:// www.blueletterbible.org/search/Dictionary/viewTopic.cfm>.

35 Simeon, C. (1833). *Horae Homileticae: John XIII to Acts* (Vol. 14, p. 582). London: Holdsworth and Ball.

36 Barnes, A. (1884–1885). *Notes on the New Testament: Acts*. (R. Frew, Ed.) (p. 356). London: Blackie & Son.

37 Carter, C. W. (1966). The Acts of the Apostles. In *Matthew-Acts* (Vol. 4, p. 695). Grand Rapids: William B. Eerdmans Publishing Company.

38 "Context." *Merriam-Webster.com*. Merriam-Webster, n.d. Web. 3 Sept. 2015. <http://www.merriam-webster.com/dictionary/context>.

39 "Condition." *Merriam-Webster.com*. Merriam-Webster, n.d. Web. 3 Sept. 2015. <http://www.merriam-webster.com/dictionary/condition>.

40 "Discourse." *Merriam-Webster.com*. Merriam-Webster, n.d. Web. 19 Sept. 2015. <http://www.merriam-webster.com/dictionary/discourse>.

41 *The Holy Bible: King James Version*. (2009). (Electronic Edition of the 1900 Authorized Version., Acts 17:1–4). Bellingham: Logos Research Systems, Inc.

42 "Dictionaries :: Dispute, Disputer, Disputing." Blue Letter Bible. Sowing Circle. Web. 19 Sep. 2015. <http://www.blueletterbible.orghttps://www.blueletterbible.org/search/Dictionary/viewTopic.cfm>.

43 *The Holy Bible: King James Version*. (2009). (Electronic Edition of the 1900 Authorized Version., Ac 9:29). Bellingham: Logos Research Systems, Inc.

44 "Dictionaries :: Persuade." Blue Letter Bible. Sowing Circle. Web. 19 Sep. 2015. <http://www.blueletterbible.orghttps://www.blueletterbible.org/search/Dictionary/viewTopic.cfm>.

45 *The Holy Bible: King James Version*. (2009). (Electronic Edition of the 1900 Authorized Version., Acts 19:8). Bellingham: Logos Research Systems, Inc.

46 *The Holy Bible: King James Version*. (2009). (Electronic Edition of the 1900 Authorized Version., Acts 19:9). Bellingham: Logos Research Systems, Inc.

47 Swanson, J. (1997). *Dictionary of Biblical Languages with Semantic Domains: Greek (New Testament)* (electronic ed.). Oak Harbor: Logos Research Systems, Inc.

48 *The Holy Bible: King James Version*. (2009). (Electronic Edition of the 1900 Authorized Version., Acts 28:23–24). Bellingham: Logos Research Systems, Inc.

49 Evans, William. "The Doctrine of Man." The Great Doctrines of the Bible, Moody Publishers, 1992, pp. 133-134.

50 Evans, William. "The Doctrines of Salvation." The Great Doctrines of the Bible, Moody Publishers, 1992, p. 152.

51 Thomas, David. "Section 111 - Acts 28:29-31 - Paul in Rome III. His Two Years' Ministry in his "Own Hired House."." *A Homiletic Commentary on the Acts of the Apostles ... Including emendative renderings, exegetical remarks ... by David Thomas. [With the text.]*, Baker, 1870, p. 480.